How to Develop Entrepreneurial Graduates, Ideas and Ventures

How to Develop Entrepreneurial Graduates, Ideas and Ventures

Designing an Imaginative Entrepreneurship Program

Edited by

Kath Penaluna

Associate Professor in Enterprise Education, International Institute for Creative Entrepreneurial Development, University of Wales Trinity Saint David, Wales, UK

Colin Jones

Associate Professor of Academic Development, Faculty of Health, Engineering and Sciences, University of Southern Queensland, Australia

Andy Penaluna

Professor Emeritus, International Institute for Creative Entrepreneurial Development, University of Wales Trinity Saint David, Wales, UK

 Edward Elgar
PUBLISHING

Cheltenham, UK • Northampton, MA, USA

Published by
Edward Elgar Publishing Limited
The Lypiatts
15 Lansdown Road
Cheltenham
Glos GL50 2JA
UK

Edward Elgar Publishing, Inc.
William Pratt House
9 Dewey Court
Northampton
Massachusetts 01060
USA

Paperback edition 2023

A catalogue record for this book
is available from the British Library

Library of Congress Control Number: 2022937631

This book is available electronically in the **Elgar**online
Business subject collection
http://dx.doi.org/10.4337/9781789909029

ISBN 978 1 78990 901 2 (cased)
ISBN 978 1 78990 902 9 (eBook)
ISBN 978 1 0353 2207 7 (paperback)

Printed and bound by CPI Group (UK) Ltd, Croydon, CR0 4YY

Contents

Contributors

Charlotte Carey is Associate Professor of Digital Marketing and Entrepreneurship Research Cluster lead at Birmingham City Business School, England.

Alistair Fee is a European Specialist in Innovation, Creativity and Entrepreneurship at Queens Belfast, University College Dublin, Swiss Federal Institute of Technology and at the European Institute of Innovation and Technology.

Gustav Hägg is an Assistant Professor of Entrepreneurship in the Department of Urban Studies at Malmö University, Sweden.

Dave Jarman is a Senior Lecturer at the Centre for Innovation and Entrepreneurship at the University of Bristol, England.

Colin Jones is an Associate Professor of Academic Development at the University of Southern Queensland, and host of the Reasonable Adventurer podcast, Australia.

David Kirby is the co-founder of the Harmonious Entrepreneurship Society and previously held Professorships at the Universities of Durham and Surrey, England. From 2007–2017 he was Founding Dean and Vice President of the British University in Egypt.

Alex Maritz is a Professor of Entrepreneurship in La Trobe Business School at the La Trobe University, Australia.

Daniele Morselli is Senior Researcher at the Faculty of Education at the Italian Free University of Bolzano.

Andy Penaluna is Professor Emeritus of University of Wales Trinity Saint David, Wales.

Kath Penaluna is an Associate Professor of Entrepreneurship at the University of Wales Trinity Saint David, Wales.

Stefania Romano is a Lecturer in Enterprise and Entrepreneurship at the University of Leeds, England.

Fátima São Simão is the Director of Development for the Arts at UPTEC – Science and Technology Park of the University of Porto, Portugal.

Silja Suntola is an EU Project Manager at the Creative Industries Research Unit at the South-Eastern University of Applied Sciences, Finland.

Margaret Tynan is a Senior Lecturer in Enterprise and Management at South East Technological University (SETU), Cork Road Campus, Waterford, Ireland.

Rebecca White is a Professor of Entrepreneurship at the University of Tampa, United States.

Doan Winkel is Endowed Chair in Entrepreneurship and Director of the Edward M. Muldoon Center for Entrepreneurship, at John Carroll University, United States.

Preface

If an idea is not absurd then there is no hope for it. (Albert Einstein)

As the alignment between entrepreneurial education, a catch all for enterprise and entrepreneurship education and the development of 21st-century skills increase, so do the demands on educators. Cognizant of a diverse learner population and certitude we are charged with developing learning, teaching and assessment that goes beyond delivering discipline specific subject knowledge, to also equipping our learners with competencies such as team working, creativity, problem solving and opportunity recognition. In turn, increasing the capacity for critical thinking and innovation, to respond to global problems, many of which have been exacerbated by the COVID-19 pandemic.

Entrepreneurial educators are presented with a plethora of academic texts to inform their approaches, and the dominant paradigm remains publications from our Business and Management Schools, and this results in critiques of a concentration on theories that "pursue conservative models rather than forward looking ones"[1] and not the 'what' and 'how' of practice that has been called for.[2]

Thus, the motivation for this book was to share the journeys of educators in this diverse educational arena, ones who work within multiple contexts, and who provide insights and observations that are forward looking, and practice led. Ideally, we seek theoretical underpinning and philosophical stances, with perspectives that any educator, new to the field or experienced, at any level and discipline within Higher Education can engage with, to reflect upon and further their own practice. The centrality of understanding education is evident, and what it means to learn and unlearn. No author claims best practice but provide practices that are relevant for their context. There are two distinct themes that have emerged, the first advocates a move away from what are termed 'traditional approaches', with educationalists understanding what it means to move from solely didactic instructional teaching (pedagogy) to more blended forms of experiential self-directed learning that embrace heutagogy.[3] This realization in itself begs an interesting question, what is traditional for whom are we talking? The second theme was sustainability, using education to help to create social, cultural and economic value.

THE ENTERPRISE AND ENTREPRENEURSHIP GATEWAY

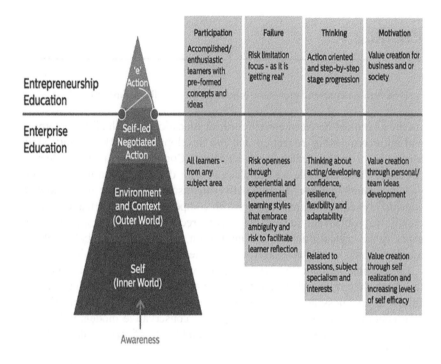

Figure P.1   The gateway triangle

The chapters are presented in three parts, capturing reflexive pieces that sit within three distinct areas of entrepreneurial learning: developing graduates, ideas and ventures. This concept is well aligned to the UK's QAA (2018)[4] gateway triangle (Figure P.1), as the authors within Part I and II observe that enterprise competencies are required for all learners, and are essential ingredients for those wishing to pass through the gateway to the top of the triangle – where entrepreneurship and the practical aspects of venture creation are demanded by learners, not assumed to simply be the right things to teach. Our Part III exemplifies this perspective.

MOTIVATIONS

What comes through strongly within all contributions is the authors' passion for developing learning experiences and environments where enterprise and entrepreneurship can flourish. This type of education can mean swimming against the tide of prior norms and accepted practices, bringing to mind the observation of Einstein in the opening statement. Perhaps this is what is meant by entrepreneurial educators, as they feel they are breaking away from the much-critiqued traditional approaches. The journeys described include challenges from fellow educators, administrators and the unexpecting learners themselves. Most educators have become adept at mimicking the risk taking they advocate for their learners – to advance their learning, teaching and assessment practice.

This passion of entrepreneurial educators extends into their forming collaborations within the ecosystem to enhance their provision. In doing so, they are not afraid to work with a hunch:

> Like any other thought, a hunch is simply a network of cells firing inside your brain in an organised pattern. But for that hunch to blossom into something more substantial, it has to connect with other ideas.[5]

Our contributions aim to inform your own hunches for practice and research, to further both your own and our community's scholarship of teaching and learning. Unlearning past and accepted practices may at first seem absurd, but read on and draw your own conclusions, based on the insights shared by those who are facing such challenges head on.

NOTES

1. See Fayolle, Kariv and Matlay (2019).
2. See Fayolle, Verzat and Wapshott (2016).
3. See the editors' most recent musing on the interplay between pedagogy, andragogy and heutagogy in Jones, Penaluna and Penaluna (2019).
4. The gateway triangle, first published in *Enterprise and Entrepreneurship Education: Guidance for UK Higher Education Providers* (see QAA (2018)), builds on the editors' original thinking published elsewhere (see Jones, Penaluna and Penaluna, 2019; Jones, 2019).
5. See Johnson (2010: 99).

PART I

The graduates

1. Influential teaching philosophies

Colin Jones

Unless we are to adopt an attitude of predestination towards scientific progress we must make some effort to equip mankind mentally, morally and spiritually for living in such a rapidly changing world.
(Brew, 1946: 11)

Our educational system is, I believe, failing to meet the real needs of our society.
(Rogers, 1993: 1)

Notions that our education systems are failing society and that society is always changing at such a rate that one's ability to learn is critically important. The chapters in this section provide excellent examples of approaches to education that seek to develop graduates with both the courage and intelligence to embrace the never-ending challenges that society immemorial has presented individuals seeking advance. A common theme that can be distilled from the contributions is the nature of that teaching philosophies the are presented alongside the nature of the different pedagogical approaches outlined.

This is very evident in the contribution from White (Chapter 2) where her childhood and relationship to her mother clearly has been very influential in framing her approach to entrepreneurship education. Drawing on the notion of a beginner's mind, White seeks an alertness in her students that would enable opportunities to be seen and understood. In a similar vein, Hägg (Chapter 3) is motivated to help students comprehend the challenges present in society that also present as opportunities. But Hägg further draws motivation from Dewey and Commenius that our students should develop a capacity to develop knowledge for future use in yet to be determined situations. Jones (Chapter 4) outlines a novel approach, that of trying to slow down the learning process so that students can find time to smell the roses. Central to this aim is developing alignment between the learner's life and their opportunities to learn. Finally, the approach of Winkel (Chapter 5) is centred around inviting his students into their human experience, getting them to reflect on who they might become by focusing on context, experience, reflection, action, and evaluation. Winkel places great importance on the solidarity, or an 'awareness that working with others is the only way to address the challenges of social problems, and a commitment to change the societal structures that negatively impact human life and dignity'. Across all of these contributions it is clear that their initial years of personal learning, and the various challenges they faced, the sense that something wasn't as it should have been, have significantly influenced the development of their teaching philosophies.

The impact of these various approaches can be clearly seen in their very different, but nevertheless, emancipatory pedagogies designed to develop entrepreneurial graduates. The competency-based approach of White is enacted through three distinct stages. With students moving from a focus on understanding the context and scope of the topic and on learning the language associated with the content topic, to being encouraged to review stories of entrepreneurs in a search for clues about where and how the ideas they have learned are found in practice. Finally, use reflection, collaborative efforts, and peer coaching/mentoring, as they become teachers to each other to develop mastery.

For Hägg, the development and use of critical reflection is a key mechanism through which the acts of knowing and doing can be united to enhance learning outcomes. The use of reflective diaries therefore acts as a bridge between theory and practice. The nature of this structured process of reflection highlights the need to assist students to develop the skill of reflecting and more importantly, being able to direct it towards the development of intelligence that can be directed to future entrepreneurial behaviour.

Building on his reasonable adventurer approach, Jones outlines an interrelated approach for graduate development. In combination, critical reflection, using an eight-step process, is combined with the use of his environment interaction framework to offer learners multiple opportunities for development. At the heart of this approach is a desire to create practical wisdom through a balancing of pedagogy, andragogy and heutagogy, through a process of academagogy.

The final contributor in this section is Winkel, whose mission is to support his students to master several specific capabilities (i.e., investigation, resilience, collaboration, empathetic action, problem-solving and Ignatian heritage). A strong social agenda is applied here, with awareness of the disadvantaged and oppressed, and notions of being action-oriented to bring about justice in society. Students are given the opportunity to 'explore the discomfort of their purpose, represented by the intersection of their passion and the impact they want to have on the world'.

What is clear across all the chapters in this section is that the contributors are change makers, seeking to use EE as a vehicle to improve aspects of society and/or the capacity of individuals to cope with what society will throw at them. The distinctive nature of each chapter serves as a reminder that EE is both not for the faint of heart, and unlikely to ever rest simply upon a standardised curriculum that offers students a predicable convergent learning experience.

As you work through the chapters in this section, also take time to embrace the candidness of the contributors, reflect on their struggles and don't lose sight of how entrepreneurial they have been in developing their approaches. Also recognise that each is offering a glimpse of a work in progress.

2. Entrepreneurship education: the journey to a beginner's mind

Rebecca White

I am still learning.
(Seneca, 65ad: from his letter to Lucilius)

My parents believed deeply in the power of education. They both believed that education was the pathway to a better life. But, they also taught us, and as my mother's willingness to go back to school after retirement from a successful business demonstrated, an education is not just about getting a good job. An education provides the foundation for lifelong learning.

My mother was an entrepreneur and I thought that would be my path as well. But life intervened and I found myself teaching at a small college after getting an MBA. Sometime thereafter, with two small babies in tow, I decided to pursue a PhD in Strategic Management. It was there that the world of academics as a career opened up for me.

My first teaching position was at a mid-sized state university in the mid-western US. After a few years, I was invited to offer a small business class and with the support of my department chair and dean became immersed in the fledging discipline of entrepreneurship. Now, 20+ years and several positions and institutions later, I realize that a degree in entrepreneurship was what I longed for so many years ago as a student. I am honored to have been a part of building this discipline that transforms lives like no other.

MY TEACHING PHILOSOPHY

As an educator I encourage my students to be a *camera* and a *verb*. Growing up with an entrepreneurial parent, I learned early in life that entrepreneurship is both a lens through which the world can be viewed and the willingness to take action. The lens is one of opportunity recognition and the action is the pursuit of those opportunities regardless of resources controlled. It is one grounded in an understanding that in order to recognize opportunities one must be engaged in and attentive to the world around them and one must take action. As an educator in this discipline, I have built on that belief system to create a context where each of my students has the opportunity to use what they learn in my classes to prepare for a meaningful career and an exceptional life based in innovative thinking and application.

However, learning is a choice, and I realize that not all of my students will choose to take advantage of the opportunities offered to them. While I do not recommend entrepreneurship as a career for everyone, I do believe an entrepreneurial mindset can be of value to anyone. A true entrepreneurial life requires an attitude and a mindset that is not for everyone. Students who embrace entrepreneurship also not only tend to embrace life with all of its challenge and ambiguity – they thrive on it. However, others find it too messy, unpredictable and chaotic. Therefore, while I do not expect all of my students to start a new venture or be business owners, my goal is that our work together serves to provide each of them with the opportunity for introspection and positive transformation.

MY CONTEXT

My teaching career began at the small college where I pursued and received my undergraduate degree. After completing my PhD, I taught graduate and undergraduate classes in strategy and then later in entrepreneurship. Today I am a professor of entrepreneurship at the University of Tampa (UT) and serve as the Walter Chair of Entrepreneurship and Director of the Lowth Entrepreneurship Center in the Sykes College of Business. UT is a private metropolitan university of approximately 11,000 students; however, I have teaching experience ranging from a large state university to a small liberal arts college. At UT, my students are primarily enrolled in the Masters of Science in Entrepreneurship (MSE) program where I teach a bookcamp style introductory course that is focused on self-assessment and the entrepreneurial journey. I also often teach a creativity and innovative problem-solving class.

My Ideal Graduate

My ideal graduate is one who is curious, maintains a beginner's mind and is willing to engage with life. In other words, I hope that my students will be a camera in life, not a picture. Being a camera, means they are curious, always observing, and willing to see what is happening around them. It means they don't spend all of their time trying to show what they already know and who they are (as in a picture) but that they are pointing outward to check out what is around them. My ideal graduate is also one that is a verb, not a noun. They don't spend all of their time defining who they are, but they focus on who they are becoming and the path that lies ahead. They become people who take action instead of spending all of their time defending who they are and what they have done thus far. This approach to life is the essence of an entrepreneurial mindset and tends to provide both opportunities and pathways to action.

As an advocate of experiential learning, I encourage my students to practice what they are learning in my class as well as throughout their entire academic career. In this way, their education becomes a bridge to their life and vocation after graduation. Over the years I have observed that those students who have an engaging and meaningful concept to work on during their coursework, learn far more than those who are working on theoretical concepts or someone else's passion. In the end, I hope that my students have not only learned basic business skills and developed the abilities necessary to succeed but have also been transformed along the way and have developed a passion for lifelong learning.

Why this Type of Graduate?

I believe the world needs more people with an entrepreneurial mindset. And opportunity recognition is at the heart of this mental map. As Shane and Venkataraman[1] put it, "...to have entrepreneurship, you must first have entrepreneurial opportunities." The graduate who is curious, has a beginner's mind and takes action is ultimately a person who not only recognizes opportunities but is also able and willing to act on them. When I talk about opportunity recognition, I often remind my students of its entomology. The word opportunity stems from Latin origin: *ob* (toward) and *portus* (port). The original term: Op-port-tu: referred to the time, before ports were dredged, when the captain and crew had to wait for the tide to rise to go in to the ports. Sailors used the phrase ob portus to denote the best combination of wind, current, and tide to sail to port. However, the only way to seize such weather conditions was if the vessel's captain had already sighted the port of destination. Knowing the weather conditions without knowing the destination was useless. Therefore, a ship was in a state of *opportunitas* when its captain had decided where to go and knew how to get there. An entrepreneurial mindset is the same. It is about having a vision (destination), paying attention to the context (wind, current, and tide) and taking action (sailing to port) when the timing is right.

My Theories of Development

The content of my courses has been influenced by a number of theories of entrepreneurship, in fact, too many to name in this short overview. As someone who has had the opportunity to be the champion of new academic programs in entrepreneurship at several institutions, I have had the opportunity to teach virtually every class in the entrepreneurship curriculum from ideation to launch and funding. Regardless of the class topic, I have learned over the years that the student who is engaged in learning via a meaningful and exciting opportunity, learns more. Students who are provided with an opportunity to learn by doing and to apply what they are learning to a project or concept that ignites not only their curiosity but also their personal interests have better grades and demonstrate more enthusiasm for learning. Like so many other educators in this discipline, I learned that experiential education works in entrepreneurship. However, with an education in business, while I had chosen to be an educator, I had never been trained in the literature of education. Thus, I began my journey to examine what educators said about experiential education and found two areas that were a fit – situated cognition and competency-based education.

DEVELOPING ENTREPRENEURIAL GRADUATES

My current instructional pedagogy has been significantly influenced by the theory of situated cognition.[2] This theory suggests that the knowing cannot be separated from the doing and that learning is enhanced when the learner is immersed in the context. The model that I have found most useful suggests that there are five components of situated learning: collaboration, coaching and mentoring, reflection, apprenticeship, and multiple practice. I first wrote about this in an article[3] that suggested that teaching entrepreneurship was more like teaching a craft, much like medicine or architecture. Over time, the theory of situated cognition has informed not only the structure of coursework but the design of new programs and even spaces for learning. For example, this theory was used as the foundation for the layout of a new 25,000 square foot space at the University of Tampa. It was also used, along with competency-based education (CBE) theory, in the plan of a new Master's of Science in Entrepreneurship at the same institution in 2016.

Introduced by David McClelland in the early 1970s, competencies were recognized as significant predictors of employee performance and success and were traditionally more associated with training than education. However, in recent years more advanced education systems have come to value it as a framework for designing and implementing education that focuses on the desired performance capabilities of the learner within this broad definitional context.[4] Whereas traditional education tends to focus on what and how learners are taught, CBE is focused on whether or not learners can demonstrate application of learning to solve problems, communicate effectively, perform procedures and make appropriate decisions within a given context. The perfect complement to situated cognition.

Stages of Development

For the development of the classes and programs I have created, it has been useful to use a competency structure model. Simply put, this is the architecture of the learning design. A competency structure begins with a list of the competencies the course or program will address. Once these have been determined, specific abilities and behaviors are then outlined for each. Once defined, specific outcomes within a clearly designed context can be determined. These pre-determined outcomes are then used to assess learning. Using CBE then allows for three stages of student development. It is important to note, however, that while students must complete each stage in order to move to the next, not all students will experience all three stages of learning for every competency.

The first of the three stages is *awareness and knowledge*. This stage is characterized by a focus on understanding the context and scope of the topic and on learning the language associated with the content topic. Interestingly, it has not always been clear to educators in entrepreneurship what it means to be a graduate of an entrepreneurship program.[5] By default, many entrepreneurship educators in the past resorted to building classes and programs based in their primary discipline – which until more recent years was not likely to be entrepreneurship.

Once the basic content knowledge is determined and learned, the second stage is *application* of these models. During this stage, students continue to be encouraged to review stories of entrepreneurs for clues regarding application, but they are also invited to begin to apply the theories they have been learning.

The third stage is *mastery or leadership*. During this stage, students are encouraged to take responsibility for what they have learned. Through reflection, collaborative efforts and peer coaching/mentoring, they become teachers to each other.

Assessing Outcomes

Using the five experiential learning modalities of situated cognition theory combined with CBE allows for the design of clear outcomes based on the three-stage model described. For example, I teach a class in creativity and innovative problem solving for entrepreneurs. This course is one of the first classes in our graduate program. The goal is for students to learn principles associated with opportunity recognition, learning from customers and from failure, and pivoting in an effort to define and refine the concept that they will use as an application project throughout the program. In most cases, this is a business venture the student has already started, wishes to pursue during the program or plans to launch after graduation. In this class, the first stage involves understanding the terminology and models associated with creativity, ideation and opportunity recognition. This stage also includes learning about the entrepreneurial mindset, that is, how innovators and creatives think, and the role of failure, resilience, perseverance and pivoting in success.

During the first stage, *awareness and knowledge*, the assignments include exams on terminology, (reflection) papers to better examine and understand how the concepts and models apply to them personally and curated stories from other entrepreneurs so that students can view the interpretation and application of these principles. To meet the goal of meaningful and applicable stories, I launched a blog and a podcast[6] of interviews with entrepreneurs. Through this program, I want students to learn how these individuals have applied these models, failed, persevered, and eventually succeeded in reaching an outcome, which may not have been the originally intended outcome, but nevertheless a meaningful result.

The second stage, *application*, involves having students research and pitch three to four concepts. The assignments for the first two or three provide very clear definition and parameters. Students work in teams (collaboration) and have several opportunities (multiple practice) to apply the principles they have learned. The subject of the final pitch is the student's concept of interest. Students are also required to find a business leader from their field of interest and shadow them during a workday (if possible) or meet virtually with them to learn more about the field (apprenticeship). Students also receive expert feedback on all concept presentations (coaching and mentoring).

Finally, students are also required to provide peer input. During this third stage students are expected to take responsibility for their feedback and to provide meaningful input to their peers on not only their concepts but also their research and assumptions (peer coaching and mentoring). Each student is graded on their ability and willingness to provide thoughtful feedback. At this stage, the students that do well have reached a level of *mastery and demonstrate peer leadership*.

Areas of Student Difficulty

Most students find the first stage comfortable because it most closely resembles their previous education. Moreover, it is during this stage that stories of other entrepreneurs, a favorite of most students, is included to demonstrate application and better understanding of the topics.

The second stage can be more challenging for students, especially those who are uncomfortable with public speaking and pitching ideas and concepts. The biggest challenge, however, at this stage is that students are unwilling to invest the time required to develop meaningful concepts. With an overwhelming amount of information available, many students depend on the top hits in a quick Google search for their business research. In many ways, this may be one of the biggest challenges we face in the education of students in entrepreneurship. Entrepreneurship is based on a series of assumptions and those must be based in knowing about the industry and world. How many times have we all had the student who declares that there is "no competition" to simply do our own cursory search and find many products and services that solve the same problem.

The majority of students are also challenged by the third stage. There are two common problems for most students during this phase. The first is again a lack of preparation. They simply do not do the work in advance that will allow them to provide meaningful feedback. When this is the case, their input is typically superficial. While someone who has deep experience as an entrepreneur or in a specific industry or field may not need to do much pre-work, most students do need to do some meaningful research on the concept in advance in order to contribute. Second, students are often not willing to take responsibility for their feedback. This is a challenge for them in part because they have grown up in a world where taking responsibility has become less common and where it is possible to voice one's opinion virtually while remaining mostly anonymous. However, to take responsibility for criticism while face to face is a challenge for most of us and perhaps even harder for students when they are providing this feedback to their peers.

My Challenges

Early on I had hopes that the combination of situated cognition and CBE could address several of the challenges we face in entrepreneurship education. Yet, while I have found the model very useful in my own teaching and in the design of programs and space at our university, we have not been able to move the discipline toward embracing this model as a shared means to advance our field and to demonstrate impact in the face of significant competition. This has been partly due to the traditions of higher education (e.g., measuring success by hours in a classroom rather than demonstrations of competencies). But it is also because we do not share a common vision and language in our field. While there has been a great deal of interest in using CBE, we have not yet realized a common structure nor a common language that would allow for an agreed-upon assessment model in the US. It is important to note however, that Europe has so far been much more successful with the effort.

Nature of Confirmation

I continue to believe that perhaps the most significant of the challenges we face as entrepreneurship educators is with assessment and demonstrating impact and value.[7] As entrepreneurship educators, most of us know that we are providing our students with information that can better prepare them to not only cope with but thrive in an Industry 4.0 world where knowing how to apply innovative thought to a world full of uncertainty, change and the lightning fast pace of technology is critical. However, learning today is also moving rapidly away from our educational institutions. Today we all know that we can turn to YouTube to learn most anything. There are many who continue to argue that a formal education is a waste of time and money for an entrepreneur. And, virtually every community is full of groups and support organizations that claim their ability to be the best provider of entrepreneurship education. How do we compete? Our discipline needs to be thinking strategically about this question and because it is a discipline-wide problem, it must be addressed collectively.

For now, lacking this common model of assessment, the confirmation comes in both "stats and stories" of success of students over the long term. Over the past several years our programs have focused more on metrics and collecting data about our alumni. The big challenge, of course, lies with defining how one measures success. Yet, however anecdotal the evidence may be, I am confident that this model has impact as I observe the transformation of our students.

SHARED WISDOM

I continue to believe this model has significant opportunity to advance our ability to assess learning in the discipline.[8] As we did at UT, this model can be used for one class, an entire program or event and even to design learning space. Furthermore, once a common structure with measures is adopted, technology can easily assess the outcomes. In the short term, this model may only be used on an individual class level. However, working within a shared CBE structure, an educator or group of educators can identify competencies, associated skills and abilities with each and define behaviors that demonstrate each skill or ability. CBE can help determine what we teach, desired outcomes and the assessment of learning and situated cognition can then inform us of how we can design learning experiences and develop assignments that will meet those outcomes.

My Development

When I first entered this field, moving from strategy to entrepreneurship, I had little understanding of the scope and direction of this academic discipline. I just knew that, after having grown up in a small business family, it made sense to me. It fit with my values and interests. As I look back at the past decades of developing programs and teaching entrepreneurship, it is gratifying to see the growth and acceptance of our discipline and rewarding to know that I have been a part of that movement.

During the early years of my teaching, our program was one of only a few that was focused on students from all disciplines, and I continue to believe that the value of entrepreneurship goes well beyond business. Thus, my own focus has moved from one of how to execute on opportunities to one of how to help discover, shape and create opportunities. While I continue to believe that success in an entrepreneurial venture (whether business or not) requires execution, I have witnessed that learning is enhanced when the learner is engaged in a meaningful pursuit. Today I am much more holistic in my approach to teaching and learning and I continue to work toward providing a learning experience that provides a more customized approach for each student. This is why I have spent as much time with co-curricular program development as with traditional classroom and degree program development.

Lessons Learned

Today I am a tenure track professor, chair, and director. I feel very fortunate to have had the opportunity to be a part of the growth and development of a discipline that is of tremendous value in today's world. I continue to believe our discipline is truly relevant. However, when I first began my work in entrepreneurship, as an untenured junior faculty member, I was strongly encouraged not to puruse the work that I found so interesting, that is, building an academic program and being a second wave pioneer in the field of entrepreneurship. I was warned that this focus was not the way to secure tenure. Building programs meant that, in addition to my faculty responsibilities of teaching and scholarship, I had to champion the design of a new program, raise money, and build alliances in the business community. The very real fear was that to engage in everything that was required to build a new program in a fledging discipline that was not yet fully accepted by the academy, would be too time-consuming without the promise of a positive outcome for my own career.

I decided to take the road less traveled. Yes, that road came at a cost, but it has also come with tremendous rewards and an entirely different set of opportunities. I was never going to be satisfied with a more traditional academic career. But the experiences I have had thus far and the people with whom I have worked over the years have been perfect for me. I have been able to be an academic entrepreneur.

My advice to others is to be authentic and true to yourself. As an educator, I can think of no other discipline that has held such opportunities for many decades and continues today to hold tremendous promise. As I write this, we are living through a worldwide pandemic. There has been significant loss and pain, but for those who choose to see the world through an entrepreneurial lens, there is also tremendous opportunity. As I mentioned earlier in this chapter, "if you want to find an opportunity, look for a problem." There continue to be problems in our discipline and in higher education. Look for them and become part of the solution.

NOTES

1.   See Shane and Venkataraman (2000: 220).
2.   See Brown et al. (1989) for a discussion on situated cognition and learning.
3.   See White et al. (2011).
4.   For example, see Bramante and Colby (2012) and Bradley et al. (2012) for application.
5.   For example, see White et al. (2012).
6.   See enfactorpodcast.com for the podcast and blog or access the podcast under the name Enfactor on most podcast platforms.
7.   See Duval-Couetil (2013).
8.   For more on this please see White et al. (2016).

3. Prudent "entrepreneurial" graduates that take intelligent action

Gustav Hägg

> Learn to do by knowing and to know by doing.
> (McLellan and Dewey, 1889: cover page)

I consider myself a troubled soul, that sometimes see too many problems in the world, especially, regarding the issue of inequality that prevails in our globalized society. A main task as an educator is to create awareness of this to students, at least that is something that I seek to do, piece by piece. I think that this striving for creating awareness and the curiosity of the unknown (i.e. knowledge or knowing that is not in one's possession) was a main motivator for me to pursue a research career and also a main driver for becoming an educator and my role as a guide to learning. There is too little space here to fully explain experiences that put me on the path towards teaching, but an influencer for viewing experiences as a main vehicle for learning took place when I was an exchange student in Denmark and a small city named Herning, where I for the first time got to experience problem-based learning and the interplay between different subject domains. Although I am still a novice in teaching and have roughly eight years of experience in the domain of entrepreneurship and business studies, I still think back on the time in Herning as a student and the approach to learning. The noviceness as an educator is far outcompeted by my philosophical and theoretical knowledge on why and how to teach. An unbalanced scale that I constantly seek to balance.

MY TEACHING PHILOSOPHY

There is a saying that goes a little bit like this, we learn through all our senses and all the parts together create a whole. My philosophy of teaching is in part borrowed from Dewey, and also from Commenius and his idea on progression, as well as current notions on experiential education where less is more and ideas of our cognitive ability; to not overload our minds. In all these different views there is a red thread that neatly is being related to the quote, *memoris acti, prudentes future*, that knowledge is built over time, we shall remember our history and the artefacts that have been culturally developed for creating a functioning and democratic society. But also, knowledge is pointless unless it is being used and applied in future unknown situations. Hence, we cannot start to climb a mountain before we have learned to tie the knot, but to learn to climb the mountain we need to gain actual experiences that includes the act of climbing. Therefore, my philosophy of teaching is to think and act in synergy, where a critical outlook on the future is needed when making intelligent acts. If not, then a climber might only climb once and learn nothing from the experience!

MY CONTEXT

Presently I teach and I am also co-responsible for a Bachelor program in IT and Economics, at the department for Urban Studies at Malmö University, Sweden. At the university the overarching teaching philosophy is challenge-based education. The context of the education is an interdisciplinary program that takes on the task of both informatics and business administration. My teaching is currently focused on undergraduate students, as in comparison to my empirical context in my PhD, where I studied a one-year master program in experiential entrepreneurship education.[1] In my teaching I have the opportunity to meet and work with the students in the first course they meet, knowledge-based marketing in the digital age, and in the third semester I have a course on business modelling as well as a course on the fourth semester in entrepreneurship which provides a good continuity in meeting and working with the students from a continuity perspective.[2] Finally, I also have the privilege to see the bachelor students in the last academic piece of the puzzle, supervising the academic thesis. Overall, the move from the master level to the initial freshmen level has been both challenging and very interesting as it has opened up to work explicitly with the role of guidance and how to address the academic learning process with novice learners.[3]

My Ideal Graduate

The ideal graduate is as the title is portraying a prudent individual that engages in intelligent (i.e. moral) action.[4] The ideal graduate of mine is one that can balance between functioning as a contributing citizen and taking moral leaps of betterment for tomorrow. It is a highly idealistic picture that might not fully be accomplished in the short term, as my underlying thoughts are based on a long-term perspective and the lifetime perspective that prudence implies.[5] But as I have always told my entrepreneurship students: To go out and make decisions always creates both positive and negative consequences in the context one is active in. Therefore, always seek to create more positive effects when making decisions than negative effects in the long-term game.

Hence, the underlying logic of this is that creating grounds for a moral course of action in the initial career has a positive long-term effect on the creation of corporate culture and a hope of steering away from the long-held ideas of profit maximization and the focus of seeing work as a function that diminishes the role of humans in the equation. So, the idealistic blueprint is in a sense hard to achieve short-term but an aspirational long-term goal. The knowledge and skills are tied to the subject area of study (today it is a mixture of informatics and business, but yesterday it was purely venture creation), but the capabilities or rather the judgmental abilities tied to the development of conditional knowledge is far more generic in scope to create democratic citizens that function in our globalized and rather entrepreneurially oriented society.

Why this Type of Graduate?

There is a balancing act that the prudent graduate is to meet. The prudent graduate is someone that can be not only a contributing enterprising citizen as the current ideas of policy governed life-long learning seeks to develop. It is foremost a slightly romanticized idea of developing a democratic citizen that not only engages in re-skilling and up-skilling for the sake of being agile and flexible to meet today's work life but instead following old thoughts of, for example, Lindeman and the basic assumptions of adult education and learning and the ideas of being able to reflect based on Dewey. Taken together, learning becomes a form of cultivation of the mind that in the words of Aristotle could lead an individual to a prudent life of deeds. Although the future is unknown and the only thing we know for a fact is that time creates change, the idea of backward looking has a given place in the academic setting. At least the insights of the pandemic have provided a glance of the importance for afterthought, contemplation and learning from our historical past. The prudent graduate is a thinking (wo)man, where the contextual boundaries of the subject area are being overridden by the attention to create self-regulated learners[6] based on a formula that blends old wisdoms and new insights on how individuals store and develop knowledge.[7] However, there is no perfect justification for the prudent graduate in the sense of hard facts or evidence-based educational goal attainment, but it is a subjective thought that has been developing over the years of studying old ideas and merging them with newer thoughts and insights on how and why learners develop knowledge in certain structured ways. My hope is that students benefit by opening up their horizon of thinking and move the needle a bit towards becoming critical thinkers and as long as they have developed from one state to another there is much to applaud, as it would mean that I have met the goal of higher education, to create critically thinking individuals that can make decisions on their own in an uncertain world that they can somewhat justify and take responsibility for.

My Theories of Development

My main departure comes from Dewey and his framework for reflective thinking, where the discussion on the empirical versus experimental method of thinking lay as a foundation. But a main source of belief comes from an early quote that is printed on the cover page to *Applied Psychology: An Introduction to the Principles and Practice of Education*, written by McLellan and Dewey in 1889, which states "Learn to Do by Knowing and to Know by Doing", where the interplay between knowing and doing takes on a more even distribution than in the more present idea of "Learning by Doing" where doing becomes the single-handed guide for learning, whilst the old idea was its interplay. As Dewey[8] writes in *How We Think*, "even when a child (or a grown-up) has a problem, to urge him to think when he has no prior experiences involving some of the same conditions, is wholly futile". The idea of the interplay where knowledge (making up theories that can be in use) plays an equal part as doing in the learning process is well illustrated in the above reasoning by Dewey and is something that has stayed in the back of my mind ever since I stumbled across the quote of McLellan and Dewey. The importance of the balanced act of knowing and doing is well integrated in the idea of developing reflective thinking and also makes sense when adding the insights made in cognitive load theory[9] on how we accumulate and store knowledge in hierarchical systems. It is also at par with the ideas in contemporary discussions on experiential education[10] where ideas on "less is more" and balancing theory and action are pertinent. Together these ideas, old and new, make up the foundation for my thoughts on moving the student towards a prudent state. Although an idealistic view that is not materialized in the timeline of only the education, but a hope of planting the seed that can in the long term lead to prudent individuals.

DEVELOPING ENTREPRENEURIAL GRADUATES

Basically, the main justification for how to tailor this process was developed over the years of being a PhD student at the Sten K. Johnson Centre for Entrepreneurship where I studied the educational process of the one-year master program in venture creation. Within the educational process my main responsibility was the reflective diaries that the student wrote every second week over the full academic year. The idea of the reflective diary was to act as a bridge between theory and practice and also to create the continuity perspective between learning experiences in the experience-based pedagogical approach that the program applies. During the years the reflective diaries[11] developed into a three-step method that I have called the diary method, which includes the reflective diary that overlooks the process of learning, and then two meta-reflection reports that take stock of the learning that has taken place and creates self-awareness among the students on their process of learning. The meta-reflection reports give the students a time to gaze back on what they have done. These two reports create an opportunity to synthesize and digest the often stressful in the moment action that is taking place during the midst of the semester. It is a form of creating space in the learning process for the students to recollect what has taken place. But this method of learning would not function well if the students had not at the same time been taking courses that provide knowledge about and for venture creation where the teaching is consisting of a mixture of theory and practice that ends with the final piece of a real-life entrepreneurial project. Within my new position at an undergraduate program, the reflective diaries are not a tool that is presently being used. Here I instead work more with the Socratic seminar, timely feedback and focused instructions and examples that can be acknowledged in the ideas of cognitive load theory. There is a mixture of theoretical lectures and more practical discussions where the use of examples and cases from reality is blended to create opportunities to develop critical thinking. However, the optimal (if that is even possible to actually find) scenery for the development of the prudent graduate lies in the continuity perspective where one learning experience feeds into the next to create the so important educative experience.[12] The entrepreneurial diary method creates a potential process to meet this continuity perspective, but there are many alternative learning activities that can be applied to create a thorough process perspective to learning, but oftentimes hard to accomplish in reality amidst a functional system where courses might have little progression in-between. But as a final note, in the ideal world I would employ the entrepreneurial diary method over the entire undergraduate program to work with the ability to develop reflective thinking.

Stages of Development

The students that go through the diary method mainly face three stages. First it is the challenge to accept that someone starts to guide how to think and also the entire idea of writing a reflective journal is for many students a bit odd and not something they want to invest time in. But by putting a lot of emphasis on first giving a lecture on the structure and importance of reflective thinking and then providing explicit examples on how to write a journal entry as well as guiding feedback in the early stages, it creates a first attempt to get the students involved and invest effort. However, some of the students only do it as it is part of the mandatory tasks to fulfil in order to get their diploma in the end and some eagerly understand the meaning and invest time in their thoughts. This is oftentimes the scenario during the first semester until they get to write the mid-term meta-reflection report where they realize the change or transformation process they have undertaken over the first semester of learning. When they look back on their learning, they realize the purpose of the reflective journal, as without the timestamps that each journal entry provides, the meta-reflection report becomes shallow due to the biases of hindsight in memory. Hence, the entries help memory, and this is the second stage of the process where they realize the potential of the diary method for their learning. However, despite this, some students do not engage fully in this process, and this is where it comes down to personal responsibility. I will not force an individual into spending time if they do not after five months believe in it. But the majority realize the potential of it and during the spring more attention is put into providing positive feedback and challenging the student's thoughts to develop their criticality. The final step is the meta-reflection report that ends the program, where they have the opportunity to gaze back on their entire year of learning and also gaze ahead and think about what the future might prevail. Hence there are stages that most likely portray many similar processes of learning, where we go from ignorance to enlightenment (a very posh way of saying that we engage in some sort of introspection to understand our environment).

Assessing Outcomes

The diary method is assessed in the final stage and the final report. It is not assessed on the level of reflective thinking as it is such an individual thing where students start on very different levels depending on their backgrounds. But instead, the report is graded on the ability to critically analyse the personal experiences and build up what can be related to the experimental method of thinking by Dewey, which comes close to the scientific method of how to make analysis. The reflective journal entries are only assessed as passed as long as the students hand them in. But the students that fail to hand in entries lose two points for each entry not handed in on the final report. This is very deliberate, as the fewer entries that a student has handed in the less potential there is to make a good analysis on one's learning process over the year that has passed. It also creates some sort of demand on the student to actively work with their thoughts over the year of study, even if they are hesitant in the beginning. In the present teaching I am more tied to using the power of essay exams to assess understanding in the students and their abilities to develop their line of thoughts. Even if I do not have the opportunity to implement the diary method, I still take inspiration by tailoring the exams based on testing the students' understanding where they get essay questions and use their own examples from real life to develop their analysis and come to new insights, where they interweave theory and practice in their answers.

Areas of Student Difficulty

First, it is to buy into the idea of writing a journal and also disclosing their thoughts and feelings about their learning experiences, about fellow classmates and the entire ups and downs of the entrepreneurial process. Giving feedback on journals can become very much like therapeutic work and I try to be very focused on giving feedback on how to think regarding their writing, to develop their reflective ability as the thoughts and feelings are sometimes much harder to address until they have grasped the underlying logic of reflection. But one main issue is to get all on board at least to have the students to give it a try. Then it is up to them to take their own decision on how much time they will invest in the process. But to not lose momentum I seek to work actively in the beginning to set the scene and make sure that everyone understands the basic idea of the journal and the five questions that it consists of (see Table 3.1). This, together with worked examples and an initial lecture, has over time worked quite well and the addition of the half-way meta-reflection report has further provided the students with more explicit understanding of the WHY of reflective thinking and the HOW of it. But student fatigue is common, and it is very much a balance when to give feedback that is motivating the students to continue and when to challenge them in their thoughts that is highly individual and requires time and effort investment from the teacher side.

My Challenges

Some of the main challenges are to get equal space in the curricula so that there is a balance between action and reflection in the learning process. Another challenge that is constant is to make the subjective and implicit ideas of reflective thinking more objective and also explicit to the students, because it is only when we make things explicit that understanding can be reaped, and our implicit insights and knowledge can be transferred to another part. But I have had the fortune to spend five years in developing these ideas that were partly in place when I started my journey as a PhD student. I have optimized and developed the theoretical arguments for the importance of reflective thinking and the three-step method, but the initial parts of having journals and some sort of final reflection report was developed before I started. So, I had the fortune to come into a process and build on some early ideas, but the challenge still remains to balance the scale between action and reflection to create a learning process where the experiences gained are truly educative.

Table 3.1   *The structure of the reflective diary*

Level	Question	Explanation
Surface	1. What have I done and whom have I met?	Highly descriptive, an opening question that triggers memory of the key events and persons that the student entrepreneur has met during the time that has passed since the last entry.
	2. Why did I do what I did?	Still on a descriptive level, but this question opens up for describing nuances in the experiences and persons that the student entrepreneur has met during the time since the last entry.
Deep	3. Observations and reflections in regard to point 1 and 2	A first move towards a deeper level where the main emphasis is on elaborating thoughts, feelings, and emotions related to the different experiences and persons encountered during the time that has passed since the last entry.
	4. Reflection in regard to (entrepreneurial) theory, linking it with point 3	The deepest level of the entrepreneurial diary. Here the student adds the layer of theory that could aid in making a synthesis of what has been experienced and the conceptual knowledge that could help with drawing new insights for future entrepreneurial experiences.
Surface (future looking)	5. What are my goals for the next week?	The final question moves back to a surface level and engages the student in looking ahead and setting goals for the future learning activities that are upcoming, this can also create an initial bridge between the diary entries.

Nature of Confirmation

There is very little evidence in the objective fashion. I have one study that triangulates the role of reflective thinking and the academic development of the students. In the study there is a connection between increased reflective ability and higher grades. Although grades are not portraying the entire story of learning, it is the best current measure we have at least. The idea that reflective thinking has a positive effect on grades is not new and has been acknowledged in many prior studies. But having clear evidence on the subjective nature of thinking and understanding the development of reflection is almost impossible. The anecdotal insights that the students make in their final reports give at least subjective confirmation that they have taken leaps of faith in the process and are able to at least start to regulate their thinking and understanding more about their own thinking. This is not to argue that by going through the diary method they will develop an ability to self-regulate, as it also demands a willingness to invest effort from the side of the student and also an ability to give timely feedback on an individual level as a teacher. It is time-consuming, and it requires resources to give feedback, but when you meet those students that also give back it is well worth it.

SHARED WISDOM

I think the generic idea of reflective thinking is applicable in all walks of life and the development of prudence is not something that is exclusive for entrepreneurial education. It is important in the entrepreneurial context due to the amount of decision making those entrepreneurial individuals engage in and the role that intelligent (i.e. moral) action has on the development of long-term corporate culture,[13] but the underlying logic of developing prudence has a very generic fundament. The role of reflection and thinking through decisions that are to be made is creating an ability to face uncertainty as Dewey once argued, since in all walks of life we face uncertainty. It is just that in entrepreneurship, uncertainty becomes apparent every day to a much higher degree than in other occupational walks of life. But the overarching framework is not tied to the entrepreneurial context alone, although there are many similar ideas that have been addressed in related fields of education. Hence, the method might be generic, but its primary context has been developed for entrepreneurs as the idea of reflection has been less addressed in it (although many prominent voices have been raised for its importance).

My Development

There are plenty of things for me to learn and every day is a new experience that feeds into the experiences I have accumulated so far. But developmentally I think the movement from master students and down to first-year students have been really eye-opening and work in a much more basic way with guidance than before. The difference in greeting new students at higher education than continuing to develop students that come to their fourth or fifth year is vast and something that has given me many new insights on how I as an educator must become more explicit and structured in what I say, how I say it and why I say what I say. In this process I take with me many of the insights from cognitive load theory (CLT) on explicit instructions and guiding examples to create some sort of stability and reduction in the cognitive load of the students. But I also bring in the insights from experiential education and the idea of addressing the WHY in learning and the idea of less is more to not overload the students. Here the ideas of Palmer[14] have played a role in the last two years on we teach who we are to create authenticity in the learning space and finally to see the students.

Lessons Learned

I am far too much of a novice to give explicit advice on how to teach. But I hope that some of the thoughts above can give rise to new ideas. But to give concrete advice I leave for the reader to interpret themselves. If we are to follow Palmer and that we teach who we are then my text can merely be a source for new ideas that the readers themselves have to develop as I am in no way experienced enough to be giving concrete advice on how to teach. So, I end with the quote that has impacted me in my thoughts "Learn to Do by Knowing and to Know by Doing".[15]

NOTES

1.   See Hägg (2017).
2.   See Dewey (1946).
3.   See Hägg and Kurczewska (2019, 2020).
4.   See Dewey (1891).
5.   See Tredennick and Barnes (2004).
6.   See Zimmerman (1990).
7.   See Sweller (2015, 2016).
8.   See Dewey (1910: 12).
9.   See Sweller, Ayres and Kalyuga (2011).
10. See Roberts (2012).
11. See Hägg (2021).
12. See Dewey and Dewey (1915).
13. See Bryant (2009).
14. See Palmer (1998).
15. See McLellan and Dewey (1889).

4. Developing slow graduates

Colin Jones

Human freedom involves our capacity to pause between stimulus and response and, in that pause, to choose the one response toward which we wish to throw our weight. The capacity to create ourselves, based upon this freedom, is inseparable from consciousness or self-awareness.

(May, 1975: 100)

My development as an educator has mirrored my own development as a person. Much like peeling back the layers of an onion, my focus on what matters, continues to reduce in terms of factors with the passing of time. Personally, my challenge has been to accept the importance of slowing down. However, an even greater challenge has been to get my students to also slow down, something I have had mixed success doing. My approach to teaching is well documented elsewhere,[1] and represents a gradual and ongoing adjustment from struggling student to entrepreneur, and then from an accidental educator to educational scholar. This chapter will focus more specifically on the latter stages of this journey, that of my quest to develop slow graduates.

MY TEACHING PHILOSOPHY

Most recently,[2] I promoted the notion of EE being aligned to developing a capacity for self-negotiated action, defined as, "the agency individuals demonstrate in directing their conscious thinking and action towards an alignment of their inner and outer worlds in order to succeed in life". Previously,[3] I have argued as follows:

good EE emancipates students from a sheltered world and allows them to explore and determine their connection to life. It is born from a field of action that differs from one individual to another. It is a process of filling out latent personalities, or, of allowing new conceptions of self and environments to be formed. It is a process of educating from within, rather than educating from afar. It is a process that fully starts when the student's life and learning are synchronised. Its aim is the development of individuals who demonstrate a capacity for self-negotiated action.[4]

While my beliefs around this thinking have not changed recently, my sense of the challenge associated with developing a capacity for self-negotiated action has deepened. So, while I see a viable pathway for student development, I also acknowledge the dominance of my students' subconsciousness over their consciousness in terms of their everyday decision-making.[5] First, I have become increasingly sceptical about my students having sufficient practical wisdom, or the ability to locate "the prudent course of action and resist the urgings of the passions and the deceptions of the senses".[6] Second, I see more clearly the struggle students have when asked to engage in critical reflection and worry about the lack of authentic depth in their inquiry and/or, the accuracy of their reflective efforts.[7]

MY CONTEXT

In this chapter, I am reflecting upon my most recent undergraduate teaching contexts. My students may arrive holding serious entrepreneurial intentions, or they may not, perhaps arriving via the route of elective subjects and/or non-preferred compulsory subjects. Either way, I am mindful of the inherent diversity within each cohort I meet. Deeper than the students' career aspirations and varying degrees of motivation are their styles of preferred learning they have developed, vis-à-vis behavioural norms and routines. For example, while students studying management, accounting, information systems and/or psychology may naturally enjoy my style of teaching, the same cannot be said generally for students I have experienced recently from the engineering or law disciplines.

One of the obvious implications of such diversity being the different expectations held about the depth and tempo of learning required to navigate the required learning journey. As an educator, my context is significantly shaped by the willingness of my students to *trust a process* designed to aid their learning. Ironically, it would seem that as I have developed my knowledge and skills as an educator, I have found less students willing to trust the process. So, my teaching context is often quite bimodal in terms of student interest and effort, which ultimately produces a divide between developing scholarly knowledge and my ability to implement such knowledge to the advantage of my students.

My Ideal Graduate

My ideal graduate is optimistic and assured. They are capable of creating opportunities for satisfaction due to their heightened awareness of (but not complete understanding) their neural processing. Such a graduate has developed a sense of which personal values matter, and how those values shape their interactions with others. This graduate has made good progress in developing the six attributes of the reasonable adventurer.[8] Therefore, they would take the time to understand the contextual application of theories, ideas and concepts. They would take the time to understand the worldviews of those they interact with. They would develop life rules based on their own personal experiences. They would embrace ambiguity, accepting the legitimacy of making decisions in the absence of complete information. They would find an uncommon interest in the commonplace. Finally, they would allow their sense of humour to be present in their day-to-day lives.

To achieve such an orientation to everyday living requires more than simply desiring the development of appropriately related attributes; it requires the student to *slow* down. In my experience, this is a very complicated process for students to engage in. They are all too often expected to produce the correct answers, devise the right strategies and/or interpret with accuracy all manner of instructions. Asking students to slow down creates a deliberate pathway from developing as a reasonable adventurer to becoming conscious of which specific schemas[9] are required (via automatic retrieval) and are needed to support a capacity for self-negotiated action. This is my ideal graduate, a student that can equally find peace within their own thinking and the circumstances of their life.

Why this Type of Graduate?

It has been said that "entrepreneurship often happens when people are on their way to something else",[10] and this has also been my personal experience. The entrepreneurial moments within our lives don't come at a specific time and/or place, and they don't come with instructions. However, they always require a number of trade-offs to be contemplated. To naïvely assume we can teach students a number of *predictable* steps that just need to be sequentially processed to ensure entrepreneurial glory, is, in my opinion, the worst form of teaching in EE. Such approaches are relatively easy for students to complete, for how can they be failed for attempting to scale the unknown via speculated actions?

What remains a far greater challenge is getting students to *slow* down and ask of themselves, why should I engage with any such steps? Indeed, will the idea under consideration advance my happiness? In the context of a life lived, entrepreneurship is a slow burn, not an out-of-control fuse that once lit, must produce fireworks galore. I wish for my student to control the size, nature and timing of all manner of events occurring in their life. More importantly, I want them to be able to make good decisions about how to proceed in life, knowing when to say no, and when to continue further into the unknown.

My Theories of Development

There are many intertwined theories of personal development/agency that have become intertwined through the development of my scholarship. As I speak to them here now, I do so with the benefit of hindsight. Therefore, the many years spent stumbling along trying to fashion together my approach is not addressed in what follows, as an extremely abridged outline of my approach. To bring to life Roy Heath's[11] reasonable adventurer approach, I increasingly draw on the classic ideas of Kurt Lewin[12] and Henry Murray[13] (amongst many others), who argued that the behaviour of a person evolves from the interplay between each person and the environments they interact with. Following the thinking of Urie Bronfenbrenner,[14] I view the desired development of each student as being "a lasting change in the way in which a person perceives and deals with his … [her] … environment". I also draw on the seminal ideas of Carl Rogers,[15] especially his provocative notion that "anything that can be taught to another is relatively inconsequential and has little or no significant influence on behaviour".

DEVELOPING ENTREPRENEURIAL GRADUATES

The pathway towards my ideal graduate is by way of developing practical wisdom, defined by Robinson[16] as "the wisdom that locates the prudent course of action and resists the urgings of the passions and the deceptions of the senses". Within this definition are two specific areas of focus. First, the notion that one can become aware of, and therefore resist, the *urgings of the passions* require the cultivation of deep and sustained critical reflection: no easy task. Second, developing a recognition of the *deception of the senses* requires that student–environment interaction is frequent and done in ways that enable false perceptions to be surfaced and reformulated. Therefore, pedagogically speaking, my aim is to get out of the way, and let my students engage with their surrounds as authentically as possible.

This is achieved through a balancing of pedagogy, heutagogy, andragogy via the process of academagogy.[17] The central focus vis-à-vis learning outcomes is upon the depth of understanding of oneself and of the nature of the elements present in the environment and the student's comprehension of related element interaction. So, there is no grade allocated to wishful thinking, often contained in speculative business plans, and none allocated to imagining solutions to (often intractable) problems that relate to other persons/contexts. Students are encouraged to bring their own interests, big or small, to the table and to work collaboratively with others to reconcile their closeness to such opportunities and the environmental challenges that are embedded with such opportunities.

The aim being to allow students to go *somewhere else*, and to reflect on the journeys that have been taken.

Stages of Development

I start from the position that within my student cohorts there exist three basic temperaments, as originally proposed by Roy Heath:[11] the hustlers, the non-committers and the plungers. The maturing of students within each of these groupings towards the behaviours associated with the reasonable adventurer varies considerably. For example, the plungers need to demonstrate restraint and pause to reflect. The hustlers need to embrace the thinking of others and focus more on the journey than the outcomes. The non-committers need to summon up the courage to get involved and connect to the process of learning.

Beyond the varying degrees of these idiosyncratic differences, students need to embrace that they themselves are the focus of the learning, rather than theories of entrepreneurship. In doing so, the stages of development align loosely (given the above stated variance) to Baxter Magolda's[18] epistemological reflection model. In order to align to the learning process, first, students need to move on from absolute knowing, accepting that there is little knowledge available to be received in the approach, and that they will not be assessed on the mastery of a large body of knowledge. Doing so, enables students to embrace the contextual uncertainty that sounds the ideas and concepts used within the learning process. At this point in time, and in conjunction with opportunities for deep reflection, independent knowing can occur through which students demonstrate independent thinking derived from the individuality of the projects. At this stage, the opportunity to also embrace the worldviews of others becomes an important factor in the development of contextual knowing through which the relationships between different environmental elements becomes clearer. Across these stages of development, students are gravitating to Heath's notion of the reasonable adventurer, in that they are developing (and recognising) an inner voice regarding how to create opportunities for satisfaction.

Assessing Outcomes

The two distinct, but interrelated areas of self and environment are the central focus of assessment. As discussed elsewhere,[19] the process of assessing the reflective self is divided equally across seven *supporting* questions (operating cumulatively). However, the reflective process starts with the students dwelling on a *primary* question that is focused on the student's learning journey.

After the students have reflected upon the primary question, they are required to deconstruct their thinking through the use of seven supporting questions.

The first supporting question is what have you learned about yourself that's new? The second, how does this relate to your values? The third, have your values been challenged or confirmed? The fourth, where is your life experience in this process? The fifth, where is your appreciation of others? The sixth, what new sources of information have you engaged with? Finally, what have you learned about yourself as a learner during this process?

Through addressing each of the seven supporting questions, students are able to reflect critically in ways that align to Mezirow's[20] process of transformative learning, using Y as a prompt around five times within the answer to each of the supporting questions to gain the depth required for critical reflection.

In terms of being assessed on the understanding of the environment, students are assessed on the knowledge of the elements of the environmental interaction framework and also their ability to apply the framework to identify new value creation opportunities.

Areas of Student Difficulty

There are two areas where students tend to experience difficulty in this approach, beyond the obvious challenge of assessments being centred on the student and not a body of knowledge. First, students typically need a lot of guidance to ensure they can use the Y process, to continually question their thinking. The requirement being that for each supporting questions, students state their position. Then, using the Y prompt, students need to ask of themselves, why (Y) do I believe/feel what I just stated, repeating this process three to four times per supporting question. The challenge here is to relax and allow the use of Y to create vertical movement in the reflection. For many students, they stay outside of the process, too focused on *justifying* and/or *explaining* their thinking rather than being content to *exploring* their thinking.

In terms of the environmental interaction framework, students are assessed in two different ways. First, while students are typically able to comprehend the 20 individual elements of framework, and often, internalise their own personal situation within the framework, the final challenge of demonstrating their understanding of the interrelated relationships between the 20 elements, is often a bridge too far. The degree of element interactivity present in the framework increases the intrinsic cognitive load faced by students. Too often, students trust their powers of memory, without accepting that the element interactivity inherent to the framework will overwhelm the working memory of most students.

My Challenges

The development of the reasonable adventurer while accepted *romantically* by faculty leaders, is, largely rejected by restrictive institutional rules and norms. In the contemporary context of (1) recruiting students and (2) decreasing attrition rates, any pedagogical approach that is demanding of students and requiring them to become uncomfortable in order to succeed, is a risky proposition. Perhaps the greatest challenge such an approach encounters is they have been developed by educators that seek to challenge students, who increasingly operate in contexts controlled by academic administrators who in practice, seem less focused on this aspect of learning.

Even if you are able to win the favour of those colleagues that control the nature of what curriculum approaches are deemed appropriate, there is no guarantee that a sufficient number of students will apply themselves to the nature of the learning process required. In those circumstances, suboptimal student evaluations of teaching produce pressure from those, that while supportive, are not always overly patient. So, it is often very frustrating to attempt to develop a particular type of student, one that is bound to be very different from those that expect to be spoon-fed in an age of student progression at all costs.

Nature of Confirmation

During the past 15 years I have had moments where the stars have aligned, and students have flourished. More importantly, in this age of post-graduation connectivity via social media, it has been very satisfying to observe the lives being lived by those students that embraced the philosophy of the reasonable adventurer and started the process of developing the required attributes. Beyond grades, the above outlined approach provides the educator with a privileged view inside the student's mind. When such a view is extended across sufficient time, deep familiarity is developed, and judgements can be made about the ability of graduates to create opportunities for satisfaction.

However, as with all other approaches to education, a multitude of other factors contribute to the life outcomes our graduates produce. As such, one must be careful not to go beyond what can be safely known. In this case, my student's reflections reveal an awakening within my students that is only possible within the context of the learning journey they have experienced. Further, where I have had multiple interactions with students across several subjects, the potential impact of this approach is easier to discern. Where I have had one bite at the cherry, I have less confidence about the transformative potential of the approach.

SHARED WISDOM

The process of reflection described above is applicable to any educational context. Once we step back to view EE less as a subject area and more potentially as a transformative process, the opportunities for the transferability of these ideas increase. My true hope is that in the coming years there will be no separate subject offerings related to entrepreneurship. Instead, all subject areas will be taught in ways that incorporate the individual life circumstances of each student within their studies. Further, that across all subject areas the requirements for post-graduate career development will be embedded into each student's studies.

I will not hold my breath, instead, I will continue to champion the importance of EE in the lives of students. Given the numbers of students increasingly enrolled in EE from all disciplinary areas, it is obvious something is missing in contemporary curriculums vis-à-vis authentic student development. The challenge we all face is demonstrating our relevance in the lives of our students. For me, that centres on practical wisdom, and the challenge of helping students learn about themselves and their surrounds; which begs the question, exactly how are you relevant to your students' development?

My Development

My first attempt at being a student in a formal setting was disappointing for all concerned. My second attempt, in a less formal, applied vocational setting produced the seeds of optimism. When I returned to formal studies as an undergraduate in my early 30s, I suffered from the inability of many educators to teach in a way that was even remotely helpful. This often-tortuous experience was a significant influence upon me deciding what type of educator I would *not* become. When I eventually settled into the role of educator in higher education, I embraced every opportunity to learn from others, and seek validation of my practice. As Parker J. Palmer[21] states, we teach who we are, therefore, clearly the most important thing to do is to learn who you are.

It is quite likely you won't like everything you find out about yourself, or your colleagues' attitudes to your approach to teaching. Don't fret, we are all on a journey of self-discovery as educators. As I increasingly embrace the person-centred ideas of Carl Rogers, I undoubtedly will be required to make many trade-offs to become even more non-directed. So, read everything you can, start with the classics, Dewey, Rogers, Erickson, Freire and Palmer. Find out who you are, and from where your practices have evolved. Leave no stone unturned, and never settle, your students' futures depend (at least in some part) upon you.

Lessons Learned

I have learned that many of the educators you will work alongside will not share your passion to go that extra mile vis-à-vis student development. This can be frustrating, especially when they take on administrative roles, perhaps to avoid teaching and/or research responsibilities, and then end up nevertheless being influential in creating the rules of how teaching can or should be performed. Never lose sight of why you teach; to help your students realise their futures. After you retire you will have a great deal of time to contemplate the failings of many you have worked with. Becoming pre-occupied with their behaviours in situ will only negatively impact the time spent with your students.

That said, I do believe we are approaching the time when educators in the domain of EE should consider starting up their own microcollege.[22] A place where "the curriculum and concentration of the microcollege is a manifestation of the mind and personality" of the educator. I can imagine a time when those educators who are best equipped to cope with the unpredictability of the forthcoming higher education landscape will be those educators who can earn a living teaching EE outside the boundaries of higher education. Nothing stays the same, our careers are full of constant change, so take on the challenge to be that change and help others to cope with and thrive in times of change.

NOTES

1. See Jones (2011, 2019) for an overview of my teaching philosophies and methods.
2. See Jones (2019: 58) for an overview of the logic of this reasoning.
3. See Jones (2019).
4. Again, see Jones (2019: 125) for an overview of the logic of this reasoning.
5. I also acknowledge the learning environment common to most higher education institutions that does not support greater opportunities for introspection.
6. See Robinson (1990: 14) for an excellent discussion on phronesis, or practical wisdom.
7. Doris (2015: x) provides an enlightening discussion of the role of reflection, noting "the exercise of human agency consists in judgement and behavior ordered by self-conscious reflection about what to think and do. Typically, this doctrine is associated with a corollary: the exercise of human agency requires accurate reflection."
8. See Jones (2011, 2019) for a full explanation of the characteristics of the reasonable adventurer.
9. See Sweller (1988).
10. See Aldrich and Kenworthy (1999). Personally, and in my observations of others, the notion that the act of entrepreneurship is more often not a secondary outcome of a prior motivation rings true.
11. See Heath (1964), *The Reasonable Adventurer*.
12. See Lewin (1935), *A Dynamic Theory of Personality*.

13.   See Murray (1938), *Explorations in Personality.*
14.   See Bronfenbrenner (1979: 3), *The Ecology of Human Development.*
15.   See Rogers (2002: 276), *On Becoming a Person.*
16.   See Robinson (1990: 14).
17.   See Jones, Penaluna and Penaluna (2019).
18.   See Baxter Magolda (1992), *Knowing and Reasoning in College: Gender-Related Patterns in Students' Intellectual Development.*
19.   See Jones (2009) and Jones (2019) for a detailed overview on how the process of individual and group reflection can be used in EE.
20.   See Mezirow (1991).
21.   See Palmer (1998), *The Courage to Teach.*
22.   See Staley (2019: 43) for an insightful commentary of the changing nature of higher education, and in particular, the looming role of the microcollege.

5. Enough is enough: put your students first

Doan Winkel

I suffered through decades as a curious student. I wanted to know why I was learning what I was learning and how I could apply what I was learning to my current existence. My teachers couldn't or wouldn't answer those questions.

My other struggle as a student was the passive learning that dominates the American education system. Like many kids, I couldn't wait for the bell to ring at the end of the school day. I wanted to be in the streets, learning about people and places and how the world worked, and honing my entrepreneurial skills. I learned by doing, and in the classroom, I never had that chance. As I emerged from the fog of my teenage years, I knew I would follow my father into academia. Not because I enjoyed my student experience, but because my student experience was years of frustration. I had a big problem, and I wanted to do everything I could to ensure future generations wouldn't have to wallow in frustration like I did. For the last decade, I brought an iconoclast perspective to the processes and systems of education. Learning can feel different than what I experienced. Learners can enjoy the process, and work on real projects that matter to them.

MY TEACHING PHILOSOPHY

For most of the last decade I struggled to adequately explain my teaching philosophy. Buzzwords like experiential and problem-based learning don't adequately encapsulate my values and beliefs as they relate to teaching. It took me, a devout atheist, stumbling into a Jesuit institution to identify the entirety of my philosophy. I don't teach. I invite students into their human experience and guide them with concern for who they become, inviting them to learn through contact rather than concepts, by focusing on context, experience, reflection, action, evaluation, and most importantly, solidarity, which is an awareness that working with others is the only way to address the challenges of social problems, and a commitment to change the societal structures that negatively impact human life and dignity.

I want students to know where they are heading, why they are going in that direction, and to head in that direction with a "capacity for connectedness". I work towards this goal with a Jesuit education approach, which is instrumental, student-centred, characterized by structure and flexibility, eclectic, personal, and a living tradition. The power of this philosophy[1] is "the method that brings about the confrontation of the person with what is true; and further, in the way in which the method of discovering the truth is itself internalized and taken from the formal learning experiences as one of its primary benefits".

MY CONTEXT

My teaching career began at Illinois State University (ISU), a large public university in the conservative Midwest. I taught undergraduate entrepreneurship and small business management courses to business students who for the most part were striving to enjoy the stability of the corporate workforce. After six years, it was decided my non-traditional and experiential approach was not a good fit for the culture at ISU, so I took a position as the John J. Kahl, Sr. Endowed Chair in Entrepreneurship and the Director of the Edward M. Muldoon Center for Entrepreneurship at John Carroll University, a private Jesuit university in Cleveland, Ohio. In this role, I enjoy teaching undergraduate and graduate students in our entrepreneurship minor and in our newly launched Master of Science in Innovation and Entrepreneurship program, respectively. Additionally, my role enables me to develop and launch a variety of extracurricular and community projects and programs to bridge the town and gown worlds for our students.

My Ideal Graduate

My ideal graduate is confident in their choices. I believe it is dangerous to encourage young people to start businesses, because, for the most part, parents and educators are unwilling to provide critical feedback and so young people pursue horrible ideas with a false sense of confidence. Instead, I believe in the power of moving students towards mastery of certain skills and abilities that an entrepreneur uses to start and build a sustainable company. In mastering these skills and abilities, any graduate can create value for any employer or partner they collaborate with.

I want graduates to have mastered the following capabilities while pursuing experiences within their sphere of purpose:

* *Investigation.* This includes looking for root causes, asking big questions, and looking at ideas and challenges from multiple perspectives.

- *Resilience*. This includes staying engaged in the midst of uncertainty/ambiguity and accessing and sustaining positive emotions.
- *Collaboration*. This includes building relationships of trust, inviting and internalizing radical feedback, and empowering leadership.
- *Empathetic Action*. This includes doing no harm, grappling with power and privilege, building empathy, and the ethics of social change.
- *Problem-Solving*. This includes systems thinking, experimentation, and customer development.
- *Ignatian Heritage*. This includes discernment, ignatian detachment, and *cura personalis* (promoting human dignity).

I want graduates to be women and men for and with others, who pursue their purpose while striving to understand and act for the rights of others, especially the disadvantaged and oppressed, by promoting the kind of justice that "requires an action-oriented commitment to the poor, with a courageous personal option".[2]

Why this Type of Graduate?

I have seen students cruise through their educational experience, and I have seen students ignited by their educational experience. I reject anything that permits students to cruise. I embrace anything that enables student ignition. This ignition happens when students explore the discomfort of their purpose, represented by the intersection of their passion and the impact they want to have on the world. In that space of purpose, the breadth and depth of student learning experience explodes exponentially.

We remember experiences. Experiences form who we become and how we make sense of and navigate our world. Students need experience to learn, and experience happens best outside the classroom. The same way that professionals develop by engaging, struggling with, and working to solve real problems, students need to encounter the same fertile ground of real problems and real people to develop their capabilities and character. When students emerge from their university experience having mastered a suite of powerful capabilities, and with a strength of character built upon solving real problems for real people and organizations, they possess the confidence to pursue the career path meant for them.

My Theories of Development

If I had to choose a theoretical foundation upon which I develop this approach, I would choose the constructivist approach of Dewey, Piaget, Rogoff, Vygotsky and others. In this vein, the learning process is construction of meaning from experience, and the instructor's role is to facilitate and negotiate meaning-making with the students. More specifically, I pursue a lean approach to teaching, coaching, guiding and mentoring. I hypothesize ways to lead students into and through experiences where they can discover who they are and what matters to them. I design experiments to quickly test those hypotheses, I analyse what happened (or didn't!) and why, and I adjust based on impact on the students. Each semester is new because I constantly learn and tweak my approach.

DEVELOPING ENTREPRENEURIAL GRADUATES

I situate my pedagogical approach as a messy experience. I do not want to talk to my students about how and when and where to apply skills and abilities I work with them to learn. I want my students to develop their skills and abilities by confronting difficult problems in their local community. Using a business model context, one example of a specific curriculum I use is that of the Experiential Entrepreneurship Curriculum[3] I developed with colleagues Justin Wilcox and Federico Mammano. As illustrated in Figure 5.1, students progress through two phases: finding a problem worth solving, and, finding a solution worth building.

Phase	Find a Problem Worth Solving					Find a Solution Worth Building				
~Weeks	1	2-3	4-5	6-7	8	9	10	11	12-13	14-15
Skill	Growth Mindset	Leveraging 1st Failure	Idea Generation	Customer Interviewing	Problem Validation	Creativity & Design Thinking	Financial Modeling	MVPs & Prototypes	Running Experiments	Pitching & Storytelling
Work As	Ind.	Temp. Team	Ind.	Ind.	Ind.	Team	Team	Team	Team	Team

Figure 5.1   Finding problems and solutions

As students navigate a semester, they vacillate between individual and team-work, and between doing and reflecting so they can internalize and solidify the learning from their experience. Students need to encounter reality throughout their journey, so instead of learning how to interview customers, they must encounter customers in a real context and practise understanding those customers' lived experience. Through this approach, students discover problems that real people face.

Once students find a problem worth solving, they progress into a process of design thinking and experimentation during which they identify a solution to effectively address the real problem they identified in the problem finding phase. Instead of brainstorming ideas for solutions in the safe confines of a classroom, students must engage with the messy context of reality to understand the current solutions real customers currently use to solve the particular problem, to understand what is lacking in these solutions, and to collaboratively and iteratively develop a solution that meets the needs of target customers.

Stages of Development

Most students begin their learning experience with me in disbelief and fear. My approach is bold, and usually different than any of my students have previously encountered. The words I use to describe the upcoming journey mostly make sense to my students, but many of them do not believe or fully comprehend what it will feel like. The first stage students encounter is tempered enthusiasm. They are excited a professor offers them the opportunity to identify and pursue their purpose while doing good for the disadvantaged and oppressed, but they don't fully believe it is real because it is an autonomy they never, or rarely experienced in an educational context.

During their first experience, I shock students by creating an experience where they quickly fail at building a solution. This stage of development is meant to confront students with their inadequacy at understanding the reality of others, and at checking both their ego and their fear so they can understand another's lived experience.

Students spend much of the semester in the next stage struggling with customer interviewing – identifying early adopters, physically finding early adopters, and extracting useful information from early adopters about their lived experience. As they progress, their confidence and excitement explode as they discover their ability to make a real impact for people facing real problems related to the student's purpose.

Students leverage that confidence and excitement to move through the stages of finding a solution worth building. They relearn how to experiment to validate ideas they believe will solve validated problems and analyse the results of their experiments. The final stage for students is storytelling. They reflect upon and share their journey with important people in their life.

Assessing Outcomes

I am unsure how to effectively assess outcomes in my approach because they are mostly transdisciplinary and qualitative learning goals that have historically taken a back seat to academic standards. Students produce evidence-based artefacts during their learning journey that capture how they confront, navigate, and grow through experiences. I have yet to find a method to effectively assess this approach. Traditional approaches of assessment fall short of guiding students on their personalized journey of self-discovery and development. A mastery learning approach[4] makes the most sense to me, characterized by "learning that is deeply personalized, student driven, based in authentic engagement, and designed to educate the 'whole student'".[5] This approach allows students to demonstrate their knowledge, skills, and dispositions with artefacts related to real problems they encounter and work to solve, and enables me and subject-matter experts to collaboratively coach students on where they need to improve.

In this approach, learners have agency over what, where, when, and how they learn, and how they tell their story to outside readers. Mastery credits include clear descriptions of what students can actually do, as well as evidence discerned from samples of their actual work. I do not approach assessment as "grading" but as feedback with radical candour. Students need a body of feedback, from multiple perspectives of related expertise, to achieve and demonstrate mastery. Shifting to what Greg Curtis calls a "grafted" assessment design approach is what I have found most accurately addresses transdisciplinary goals alongside disciplinary ones.[6]

Areas of Student Difficulty

Students initially struggle with most of my approach. My job is to coach them through the journey, so they understand why we are on the journey, what they need to do to progress on the journey, and how they are progressing along the journey. Often, students struggle to fully engage. My learning experience is scary to them because it is very real. They encounter real people who are struggling with real problems and who want effective solutions to those problems right now. They cannot read a book and succeed. They cannot study for a test and succeed. They cannot remain in the safety of a classroom or behind a screen and succeed. There are no right and wrong answers. Everything is messy because it is real, and it is ambiguous. This approach is not how most students are comfortable learning. Conceptually, they struggle to process what is happening. But they quickly understand and buy into the power of this approach because we start off discussing past experiences that most impacted them and helped them grow, and they come to the realization they are embarking upon a similar experience but with the wrinkle of using their time and talents to help others. The fear of the unknown rather quickly transforms into almost giddy excitement.

The most important way I help my students is by establishing trust. I do this from day one by being radically transparent about why I chose this approach, about my fears for them, and about my commitment to helping them understand the who, what, when, where, why and how of our collective experience. I use previous student and stakeholder voices to share the impact of this approach; because it is such a departure from the norm, students need to hear more than my perspective to believe in their ability to achieve success.

My Challenges

My main challenge is balancing reality with responsibility. I need to create experiences that have a positive impact on my students and on the people with whom we are engaging. This requires I be extremely adaptive as I juggle the needs of very different stakeholders (mostly privileged college students and disadvantaged individuals in our local community). I spend considerable time learning from the experience of a variety of community activists and entrepreneurs who have a long history of engaging with similar populations we are working to engage.

Another big challenge I face is maintaining the energy and availability to effectively coach my students. My students initially require considerable emotional support as most are fearful of their ability to succeed in my approach (i.e., get a good grade). As we progress, students require considerable guidance to contain their excitement and remain grounded in understanding the lived experience of the people we are working to serve.

Nature of Confirmation

My confirmation comes through student reflection and through seeing the change in the experience of those we are serving. Throughout the semester, students reflect on their experience through a variety of written and video assignments. I see the growth in their confidence, in their ability to investigate, collaborate, take empathetic action, solve problems, and be resilient, and in their ability to understand their place, value, and purpose in the world.

My other confirmation comes through understanding how the experience of those we strive to serve changes. Sometimes the change seems outwardly miniscule at best, but the real change is huge and powerful because the people we serve share their gratitude and increased confidence because people view their experience as worthy of investing in.

The last piece of confirmation comes from graduates. Many graduates take the time a few years after graduation to let me know how valuable the experience is in helping them navigate life after college, and how often they use skills and abilities they developed during the experience to produce value for others in their professional life.

SHARED WISDOM

My approach is not an easy one. It is not easy to implement, because it is essentially an independent study with every student, and involves the complexity of emotional, mental, and spiritual growth. It is not easy because it very blatantly challenges everything about our current education system. But through all the difficulties and risk involved in this approach, it is what I believe is the best approach to developing entrepreneurial graduates who can create sustainable value for others. This approach to engaging students, rooted in the Jesuit tradition, creates impact anywhere students are learning, because it situates them in their own and others' lived experience.

Lessons Learned

Education as a system is allergic to innovation. Innovation doesn't necessarily mean we have to discover a new horizon. In discovering the centuries-old Jesuit pedagogical tradition, I stumbled into a powerful path to innovating the educational experience of my students. The great challenge for educators and administrators is how to enable this kind of approach that transforms our students and the individuals they seek to serve. Reward systems need to be expanded. Teaching evaluations need to be reimagined. Drastic change requires courage, from those implementing it and from those benefiting from it. My challenge to faculty is to believe in your students and put their future first when considering how to structure your next course.

NOTES

1. See Newton (1977: 19).
2. See Kolvenbach (2000: 6).
3. See https://teachingentrepreneurship.org/exec/ to access further information on a host of curriculum resources.
4. See https://mastery.org/.
5. Ibid.
6. See https://mastery.org/assessment-series-2-2/.

PART II

The pre ideas

6.   Creativity at the heart

Andy Penaluna

When thinking about developing entrepreneurial learners, we are pressed to think of starting points, then to challenge our own assumptions and ask, what do we need before that? The UK's Quality Assurance Agency's Guidance includes a diagram called the 'Gateway Triangle',[1] which helps us to think about a learner's 'long' journey from basic awareness towards interaction with the outside world, and then from negotiating their learning to decision time, 'shall I become an entrepreneur'? The European guidance framework 'EntreComp'[2] considers moving from dependency on the educator to self-direction and autonomy of thought, and from working in simple contexts to complex and ambiguous environments.

Whenever we look at these and similar frameworks, and whether we use the words enterprise, entrepreneurial or entrepreneurship, there is an assumption that creativity is inherent in the contributions to this section. As Fee (Chapter 7) citing Seelig, suggests, 'Creativity is the heart of invention', and what is entrepreneurship without invention? He goes on to point out that 'creative thinking makes things better, cheaper, lighter, simpler, faster, recyclable and more functional'. Morselli (Chapter 9) finds himself compelled to seek out novel solutions and things that can be modified to become more effective. Jarman (Chapter 8) suggests that creativity is central to seeking out alternative futures, while Tynan (Chapter 12) quite simply relates creativity to potential.

If we were asked to identify where expertise in creativity lies in an educational context, it is unlikely that a business or management school would be the first place we looked. However, as Romano and Carey (Chapter 10) illustrate, humanising education and enabling learners to make their own decisions is at the heart of transformational learning, and at the heart of transformational learning is shifting negative experiences into learned new ways of doing things. They note that what they call 'traditional education' may be hindering development, and that co-creation can be a tool for developing active participation. This is something they practise as well as preach, and openly borrow from other disciplines.

Tynan has made this her goal and has undertaken significant research that compares educational approaches developed by colleagues in different departments in Ireland. In her journey of discovery, she explains that design education has proven to be a useful source of inspiration and is especially helpful during the creative phase of opportunity recognition. She cites the work of Penaluna and deliberately encourages her students to think wide before making decisions, as is the dominant paradigm in many creative programmes of study. Penaluna's journey is the other way around, as his experience as a designer led him towards a realisation that few enterprise or entrepreneurship courses had developed the in-depth insights that design educators use to develop innovators whose sole purpose is to solve other people's problems. He draws on distinctions found in assessment of learning, asking when educators' assessment of learner performance is merely implementing the known, because it relies on pre-existing knowledge as opposed to the exploration of potential innovations that are as yet, unknown.

Shared comprehension of these matters is very much a matter of stimulus, and as Morselli explains, a sense of initiative and agency requires a personal stimulus that comes from the learner and goes beyond any stimulus that an educator can provide. Becoming a process stimulator is a task he identifies, as a 'change effort' requires interaction with others. Jarman concurs, stating that 'a rich and diverse diet' can be stimulated by speakers, informal guests, mentors, judges and clients who brief the learners, once again using the methods developed in design. This of course requires emotional engagement, and an educator who is prepared to tolerate ambiguity and uncertainty in order to guide students towards their own answers.

All of the authors in this section advocate experiential learning, and as Fee points out, when we set out to do something different, we become curious, developing new skills and making new discoveries – squeezing the learner's minds to think through the stimulus of unusual and unexpected inputs. As an engineering educator who works through poetry, as opposed to learning through anticipated texts from engineering, he again espouses the causes of those who experiment alongside their students, becoming a role model as well as a deep thinker who guides the process. Daydreamers and imaginers can become self-starters as Romano and Carey illuminate and can lead to an ethical disposition that cares about the impact of a new venture as well as preparing them for the dynamism of change that they are likely to encounter.

This is a preparation for lifelong learning and as Morselli explains in some depth, goes way beyond the metaphors of learning as acquisition and learning as participation, enabling learners to challenge norms and to actively seek out alternatives that may bear more value. This may be more challenging than is first realised, and as Jarman suggests, whilst students revel in the opportunity to explore, they may also feel threatened by ambiguous situations where clear pathways of intent need to be forged, not borrowed. Tynan introduces the consideration of time, as this is slow learning that is difficult and immediate answers are rarely good ones. She suggests that the scaffolding that is required is dependent on past experiences and educational engagements, and that managed stepping back is essential if students are to get past the immediately obvious, but poorly considered argument.

Another denominator that can be found in these chapters is the ability to reflect on ones' actions and thoughts, which Tynan describes as especially supportive when learners attempt to sell their idea or solution. Simply put, they have investigated in depth, considered many options and thus, can effectively argue their choices.

There are many, many links and connections between the contributing authors, however, there is much more to discover in their shared personal insightful texts than in this brief overview. As we know, the creative amongst you will already be making many new connections of your own, seeing new alignments and recognising emerging patterns of thought. Before you move on, please consider your own brief recap when reading this section, and surface your own creativity by making connections between the texts that may have been missed in this introduction.

NOTES

1.   See QAA (2018).
2.   See Bacigalupo et al. (2016).

7.   Creativity on a skateboard

Alistair Fee

The biggest failures of our lives are not those of execution, but failure of imagination.
(Seelig, 2012: 4)

We are all inventors of our own futures. Creativity is the heart of invention.
(Seelig, 2012: 4)

The most successful scientists are not the most talented, but the ones who are just impelled by curiosity.[1]

My father was a dedicated educator. He taught in the great outdoors as a farmer and businessman whose attention to detail was intense. He taught me to plough fields and leave furrows that were perfectly straight, using aligned bamboo canes as a guide. He taught me the importance of planning, leadership, strategy, thinking, and designing the perfect business outcome.

At university I studied Commerce. In my first decade of work I was involved in buying and selling electronics, anti-aircraft missiles and textiles. This involved research, business proposals, international offset arrangements and understanding economics. Two experienced international business colleagues educated me in a cornucopia of business skills. I became an educator by accident, when my university asked me to run a short course on marketing for Masters of Engineering. The course lasted for six Wednesdays. Students found it meaningful, and relevant so it was extended for 22 years!

I am committed to doing things differently in pursuit of doing things better.

I quickly recognised that teams and companies must be agile and flexible, bold and daring. They must travel beyond their normal horizons to find ideas. I became curious about everything, and relentless in seeking out techniques, and methodology. By challenging all the norms of business, I created my own unusual, and insightful approach to education.

MY TEACHING/FACILITATION PHILOSOPHY

Pedagogy is the art, science or profession of teaching and understanding education. There is no such thing as exact art, nor exact science. I enjoy teaching and facilitating groups of people who want to learn more. I am really interested in facilitation of thinking. Thinking is necessary, is allowed, and people must also think aloud. To think for oneself one must have a degree of knowledge usually learned by reading books, papers, and lecture notes. We must blend collected and experiential knowledge, combine it with our own point of view and move forward.

I start with the fundamentals, including the texts of Kotler and Porter. In my library of over 1000 business books, titles that stand out include, *Brains Versus Capital, Disciplined Entrepreneurship, Innovation Leaders, Why Not, The Art of Innovation, Don't Compete; Tilt the Field*. Each book is loaded with techniques and strategies around creativity. The fundamentals take us to a point where theoretical study meets real life. I introduce students to a complex and chaotic world in which nations, cities, universities, and companies compete for attention. If it is all about winning then these organisations are competing to be the best by rank, influence, or income.

In reality, it is about being successful. When we set out to learn, we must do it to make meaning and add value. We can make meaning in our research, science, specialist subject business or life; when we build on the shoulders of giants, we advance humanity. With young engineers I like to explore technology and design, in all its forms; in all its artfulness and beauty so that by thinking broadly we create, collaborate, and recombine ideas to make things better.

MY CONTEXT

Taking our minds from book to business requires us to put into context many subjects. The purpose of art, biochemistry, design, engineering, literature and language, medicine, and music, is to enhance society. Consider, for example, a baby stroller – a wheeled conveyance with a very demanding passenger. The role of the engineer is to make it strong enough, small, or large enough for purpose, light enough or heavy enough to cope with cobbles, pavements, public transport, and forest paths.

The role of the designer will include making it colourful, the correct size for parents of all heights, ergonomically pleasing and delightful. Others will brand it, include silent smooth bearings, add textiles that keep the baby warm or cool, safe, and secure, measure its temperature, heartbeat, movements, bodily functions and even play music, videos, or sounds to induce sleep or mental genius. Creative thinking makes things better, cheaper, lighter, simpler, faster, recyclable, and more functional.

Cross-pollination allows us to transfer ideas from a baby stroller to an aircraft seat, wheelchair, an armchair or even to a bicycle. A collaborative design team can take all of the elements required and turn them into a well-formed, functional, finished product.

My Ideal Graduate

I enjoy working with graduates who are committed to their subject. Those with deep interest in their subject, are prepared to spend time acquiring a more complete understanding of it. My task is to encourage them to take a wide view of lots of additional things. There is no such thing as an ideal engineering student. Students are all different; variously interested in many aspects of infrastructure, aviation, the auto industry, medical devices, oil and gas pipelines, body sensor systems et al. Outstanding graduates have curiosity, a willingness to explore, be adventurous, and make mistakes. They are prepared to include art, poetry, and music in their persona.

The *Poetry of Victorian Scientists* by Daniel Brown blends poetry, science and nonsense. In chapter 6 of his book, Dr John Tyndall talks about scientific use of the imagination. James Clerk Maxwell writes about puns, analogies and dreams, all of which helped him when writing his Theory of Electromagnetism.

The poet Keats studied medicine, surgery and pharmacy at Guys Hospital, he graduated with a full Apothecary licence. He also had an interest in astronomy. This helped him to understand complexity, possibilities, beauty, and by recombining his knowledge it made his poetry greater. Engineers who recombine knowledge from elsewhere, become greater.

When we are prepared to study new and unusual topics, we often find new connections. When engineers, cardiologists, software writers, and drama professors meet over pizza to discuss micro medical engineering, ideas flow in abundance, blend together and unexpected, new, brilliant outcomes occur.

I know because I tried it! In the context of pedagogy, andragogy and heutagogy I am trying to create multifaceted minds that are prepared to go further, look more carefully, are restless, and rarely contented. My top graduates really embraced the benefits of such a method, and always surprise me with wonderfully creative ideas.

Why this Type of Graduate?

In business I've had many Eureka moments and a few commercial disasters. The Eureka moments occurred when ideas from different sectors collided. A definition of insanity, often attributed to Einstein, is doing the same thing repeatedly and expecting a different result. There is a wonderful Stanford University quotation; 'When something breaks, don't buy a new one; fix it'. I want graduates to observe, find different ways of fixing and improving things. They will not be successful if they do it the way everyone else did it the last time. All graduates must be well versed in the logic of curiosity. Curious graduates tend to try things that are illogical. We must not only learn how to think differently, but we must also be prepared to try new things.

The underlying logic is this: when we set out to do something different, we discover new things and additional skills. This logic has served me well in 22 years of teaching Masters of Engineering students. Students who engage in curious and creative techniques are always better at design. Nearly all engineering students struggle with creativity when it is first presented to them. They have spent many years in the exacting world of mathematics and physics; have spent much time trying to find the right answer, to be correct and exact. The world of business is never fully correct nor exact. Creativity reminds us that there is not just one answer to anything. There are always options, choices to be made, and different possibilities.

My Theories of Development

I'm not a full-time academic, though I am a Fellow of the Higher Education Academy and a very deep thinker. Although very practical, I start with mixed elements from Michael Porter, Osterwalder and Pigneur, and Peter Fisk, I then connect with the practices of John Mullins, Seth Godin, Chip and Dan Heath, Robert Sutton, Tom Kelly, Simon Synek and many others. Current business magazines and national newspapers keep it fresh.

We discuss the business activities of successful and failing companies plus curious, creative, design-driven companies. We analyse unusual thought leading and growing businesses. You take any mind, tease it and squeeze it with unusual inputs, ask it to be relentless, bold and daring; then demand that it uses creative imagination, and it will do it every time. Provided it is willing, and believes that it can, it can become unstoppable. I am constantly surprised by the creative capacity of individuals and teams when they throw out the rulebook, cross-pollinate ideas, collaborate together, and dare to try new approaches to challenges.

DEVELOPING ENTERPRISING CREATIVE THINKERS

My approach to creative thinking mostly avoids traditional texts. Big picture thinking is not adequately described in foundational texts, rather it comes from within each of us, yet it must be released. Putting magic design into any product or service requires more than basic knowledge of a subject. T-shaped thinking, multiplied by imagination, delivers products and services that are well crafted, intuitive, and better. To be radical we must be different. I have written many case studies based on simple everyday products. A few examples follow. A cup of coffee is a fairly simple thing to make. A perfect cup of coffee is different, requires more thought and delivers a better experience. Perfect coffee requires more granular detail; planning, quality, authenticity, design, and delivery in order to delight the taste buds.

Personally, poetry makes our minds think differently as well. I have collected an anthology of poems with business resonance.[2] When introduced to poetry, many graduates initially feel uncomfortable; they think that literature, art and music serve no purpose in their pursuit of engineering excellence. However, reading and writing poetry makes graduates more insightful, and willing to mentally stretch. Their neural networks are enhanced. Poetry also enhances imagination, resulting in better report writing, shorter sentences, and more accurate vocabulary. Art enhances visual presentations, corporate pitches, business brochures and website design. Graduates who use both sides of their brains are much more creative.

Stages of Development

The first response to my teaching method has included: eye rolling, a few sighs of hopelessness, nervous laughter, raised eyebrows and one graduate even asked if he was in the right class! Ripples of interest and surprise also occur. Students react well to something non-traditional, vibrant, new, and giddy delivered with a sense of purpose. The joy of a fresh approach comes later. When I first ask graduates to write poetry they hesitate. Then they try; try again and become better.

My goal in teaching is still to be deep and meaningful. John Burnside, *Daily Telegraph*, 18 January 2012 wrote:

> Poetry is central to our culture. It is powerful and transformative. Poetry has changed the way I look and listen to the world. Poetry contains secret knowledge. Poetry makes us think and opens us up to wonder. It can be astonishing. Poetry renews and deepens our imagination and makes our minds more capable of flexible, lateral thinking.

I agree with him.

One scientist, I recall, complained that poetry should be removed from the course. She returned to her laboratory, read old poetry books, wrote her best project proposal ever, and raised a very large research grant. She blamed me for her success, with a wry smile, "Poetry made me think differently, and write better", she said.

The lyrics of popular music are poetic. Rock music can release powerful emotions and energy. Music of all types will ease tension and enable new thinking in the quietest, and deepest of all graduates. It is another art form. Graduates who relax, have fun, and are curious about more things will always discover wonderful new connections. My approach builds confidence, gives permission to be bold and daring, radical, and relentless; helping us to become remarkable.

Evaluating Outcomes

Can creativity be evaluated and measured?

It is impossible to describe art; it must be seen.

Impossible to explain music; it needs to be heard.

Art is in in the eye of the beholder. Our preference for landscapes, portraits, abstract art, the colour blue, a blank canvas varies over time. Great art can be colourful, complex, imponderable, muddled, harmonious, simple, and more.

Creativity is also in the eye of the beholder.

Creativity can be observed when graduates find new points of interest, and when they connect with new ideas and people, when graduates are enthusiastic, energetic, excited, filled with wonder. It can be evaluated by observing levels of exploration into technology and human interface.

I look for graduates prepared to deeply investigate problems and then use innovative techniques to solve them. I evaluate graduates over time, from when they first identify a problem, through idea creation, reconnaissance, prototyping, design, development, delivering and delighting the end user.

A graduate must identify the following:

- What is the problem?
- Why does it matter?
- Who cares?
- What idea will fix it?
- How will they solve the problem?

The overall problem-solving process requires them to talk to many experts, potential customers, specialists, users, manufacturers, scientists, unusual others, and competitors. Creativity is obvious when you see it at work. It requires knowledge of what already exists, an evaluation of the idea, the market, available technology, emerging technology, and design options. Often there will be an additional quirky and unexpected ingredient. Creativity adds value and should have purpose. I evaluate creativity by mixing aspects of an idea team insights, incubation, implementation, design and delivery of a new product or service.

Areas of Student/Graduate Difficulty

Students often tell me that they are not very creative. Others falsely believe that they are creative and come up with one initial idea, convinced that the idea is brilliant. They will design around their first and only idea and no matter how many hurdles they encounter, continue to believe that the first idea will get to market, if only they can find the right customer.

Another common difficulty is an inability within a team to combine their skills, and strengths. By cross-pollinating their thought processes, individual ideas and knowledge, a fully integrated team will swiftly iterate the product design and business plan, improving it at every stage. Sometimes an over-zealous team member takes the role of dictator, forcing the rest to follow one solitary route. Some teams contain a member who is content to contribute little, be a sleeping partner and quite happy to accept a shared mark at the end of the year. University teams sometimes contain a quiet, deep thinking, gentle member who is reluctant to offer an opinion even though their ideas have much value. This silent knowledge must be teased out at regular tutorials or project meetings. Good inter-team communication is key.

I maintain momentum by having regular team meetings in which I, as a mentor and corporate adviser, ask probing questions about the project. I also ensure that each student is regularly tasked with a particular part of the project.

Most engineering students like the technology, design, and customer research. Fewer are fans of finance and marketing. Careful coaching in all of these elements teases out these difficulties and it is usually possible to create a good team spirit.

My Challenges

My approach has evolved over time. Traditional business courses used to be very theoretical. However, down on Main Street, business is not theoretical; it pays to be streetwise, tuned and buzzing with many business skills, flicking from one to another as the need arises. Traditional education is usually linear. My approach is not. It requires everyone to cross chasms in their minds. Almost everyone is prepared to give it a try. Faced with uncertainty and the complexity of markets a creative, innovative mind will cope better than a theoretical one. Poetry, and art, the big picture, horizon scanning, new funding techniques, and T-shaped thinking enable our minds to change gear quickly.

The AHA! moment arrives when this happens; then unrestricted thinking is released. You cannot become really creative by only reading books about it. You cannot write a convincing business plan by only following a model from a management book. You must do it for real, get into the marketplace, network meaningfully and learn as you go. Life and business are edgy, we must take chances and learn to fly by jumping.

Nature of Confirmation

By way of confirmation that my approach is effective I can refer to several reference points. Student course satisfaction feedback has consistently been very good or excellent, and anecdotally, feedback continues over the years.

One former graduate, now a senior manager in a multinational company wrote to me recently telling me that she had forgotten everything she had learned at university except for the content of my course. Ten years later, she wrote me a five-page letter outlining five different aspects of the course content that she is still using today.

My course content, with my own particular quirky delivery style is much used in executive education courses at some of the top business schools in the world, but I call it "Marketing Innovative Technologies" whereas it should really be called "Creativity on a Skateboard". It is active and effective, real and reflective, keeps our minds busy.

The purpose of creative education is to transform minds forever, like a sprawling River Delta where ideas meet and trade is multiplied, it is much used and sought after by industry, government departments, and academia. A multifaceted approach to the human mind, educating our brain to use all its senses, teaching ourselves to be idea hunters rather than matrix followers is the best way of being competitive, revolutionary, and remarkable.

SHARED WISDOM

Thinking differently is not being confined to university lecture theatres, yet every organisation can benefit by being creative. My approach is not new, but my style is new, and to my students my delivery is unique. My approach recognises that lifelong learning in creativity and innovation can keep our minds agile; it is possible for every societal niche to be enhanced.

There are many super creative spaces in the world: Hasso Plattner Institute, Design School Stanford, Aalto Venture Garage, creative hubs in Berlin, London, Dublin, Munich, Amsterdam to name a few. Some global companies have their own innovation universities within their organisations. But consider this, many primary school teachers are full of creative pedagogy. It becomes harder to be creative at secondary school level as competition for league table rankings takes over: schools are measured by their exam marks rather than their creativity.

I am even creative in my garden. I constantly mow my lawn in various patterns, try different tools on joinery projects in my garden shed. I have managed to find 22 different ingredients to put on a lunchtime salad to create a feast for my fingers, eyes, nose, ears and tongue. Creativity reduces as we get older, unless we nurture it so avoid your daily treadmill – jump off and try something new.

My Development

My personal journey of creative thinking and innovation has evolved over 20 years. I started carrying out simple experiments of thought with students. A well-known exercise explores what else a paperclip can be used for. Answers from 100 options include a toothpick, a lock pick, jewellery, or a bicycle chain.

My exercises became more demanding both for me and my students. What are the six purposes of grass? There are many more than six. List everything in the room – walls, floor, ceiling, carpet, desk, laptops, mobile phone, door handles, hinges, screw-nails, hope, ambition, inspiration, compassion, collaboration, and ideas. This exercise is always mind stretching. I stretch my own commercial philosophy by removing barriers; not being limited by normality, rather to break out. I had become a prisoner of doing well; rather than doing differently, and that has made all the difference. Creative thinking requires us to ignore perceived boundaries, soar into the stratosphere and explore beyond the horizon. That is what great scientists, engineers, artists, and poets have been doing for years.

Lessons Learned

On a sunny day in the Alps, my Stanford Professor trekking companion asked me if I was ready for another academic year of creativity and innovation. I told her that I was quite content and ready for an ideas-filled year. Aghast! She told me that I must never be content, there is always more to be done and achieved.

If facilitators are to create a worthwhile and vibrant future, they can only build it on the ideas and flexible minds of others. We ourselves must practise being creative, question everything and let our imagination run riot. We can all easily come up with one or two ideas and think we are done. I have never been content since trekking in the Alps. I continue to grow my network; my mind has fewer limits and when I come to a barrier, I work diligently to find a way past it.

Creativity is fun. I am no longer bound by pedagogy. I have become "Boundless". Like the blue paintings by Yves Klein, bit by bit I have built a creative space, sharing my insights, and kaleidoscope of ideas, mentoring individuals and teams from everywhere. Creative thinking will enhance your life and the lives of those around you. Try it, just to see what happens, and maybe get inspired by texts like the ones in my notes section below.[3] Above all, enjoy the journey.

NOTES

1.   This quote is often attributed to Arthur Leonard Schawlow following his 1981 Nobel prize in physics for his contributions to laser spectroscopy, but see also Barton Rabe (2006: 77).
2.   Some favourites of mine include *Ithaca* by Constantin Cavafy, *The Golden Journey to Samarkand* by James Elroy Flecker, and *The Music Makers* by O'Shaughnessy.
3.   All the following are excellent sources of inspiration; *Non-Stop Creativity And Innovation* (2001) by McLeod and Thomson; *Imagine: How Creativity Works* (2012) by Lehrer; *How to Get Ideas* (2007) by Foster; *Hegarty on Creativity: There Are No Rules* (2014) by Hegarty; *Seeing What Others Don't* (2017) by Klein; *Creating Breakthroughs at 3M* (1999) by von Hippel, Thomke and Sonnack; *Making Ideas Happen* (2010) by Belsky; *Sticky Wisdom* (2002) by Allan and Kingdon; and *What If? Serious Scientific Answers to Absurd Hypothetical Questions* (2015) by Munroe.

8. Creative fitness

Dave Jarman

Chance favours the connected mind.
(Johnson, 2010: vii)

I had decided to be an educator of some kind by the time I applied for university. I am not sure why I had decided that, but I have always loved being in education and I have been here for almost my entire career, albeit in a variety of roles. My undergraduate degree was in English Literature and Classical History, which was as close to a degree in mythology as I could get, and my Masters' degree is in Myth. Mythology is a creative interpretation of the world, which builds a system of explanations, which in turn enables people to tell and justify their own stories within it, and that mix of imaginatively explaining ourselves has always fascinated me.

I have been a skills trainer, personal development coach, start-up coach, freelance training facilitator and led a Careers Service before my current academic role in entrepreneurship education. I have been running workshops in creative practice for over a decade in different roles. I have come to realise over time that I have always followed my interests from stepping-stone to stepping-stone and built out my own narrative step by step; I have rarely performed any detailed calculus or strategised too far ahead. I believe that creativity is critical in this context for helping students identify the different stories that they could tell about themselves as they identify and consider the steps they might make (or sometimes explain to themselves in retrospect).

MY TEACHING/FACILITATION PHILOSOPHY

My teaching philosophy is that diet plus exercise gets results. By diet in this context, I mean what are you feeding yourself and your students; is it nutritious? Is it diverse? Does it enrich and fuel your work? If 'garbage in equals garbage out' what are you feeding yourself and your students to produce a successful or creative outcome? Students do not produce new and innovative answers if they are fed an uninspiring diet.

An improved diet by itself does not make you fit. You need to exercise to gain flexibility, stamina and strength. Creative practice is no different; how can

I stretch my creative and intellectual muscles in new ways to gain flexibility, how can I push myself to keep going in adverse circumstances, or build my capacity to undertake bigger or bolder projects? Results is not finding a 'right' answer, or even lots of answers, it's about finding diverse, surprising, and transformative possibilities.

To both explain and extend this metaphor of my teaching philosophy I always to try and expose my students to a wide array of material from academic and professional sources, drawn from different domains, and pull on their own experiences too to further enrich the learning materials available in the room. This rich and diverse diet will be supplemented by external guests as speakers, mentors, judges, or clients who will both add to the diet and provide 'stretching' exercises as the students try to engage different audiences. I am also a wholesale subscriber to experiential methods of learning, the students need to *do* things: primary research, prototyping, pitching, working together to solve problems, and this provides more demanding and emotionally engaging exercise than rhetorical reasoning.

MY CONTEXT

In my current role I am a Senior Lecturer in Entrepreneurship at the University of Bristol, teaching across undergraduate and postgraduate programmes as a unit and programme-level director. I teach a mix of design-thinking, human-centred research practices, and new venture-creation units to students at all levels of degree-level study and across all disciplines; from first-year History and Music students, through finalist and master's students in Lifesciences and Medicine, to PhD students in Engineering and Mathematics. In all these settings I am providing students with the tools to solve problems and to identify, evaluate, and develop opportunities. I regard creative practice as an essential tool for all those groups and contexts.

Creative practices might be foregrounded in some teaching and assessment contexts and merely background in others but in all those instances I will be trying to both enrich their diet and exercise their muscles in new ways. For example, our first-year students electing to study Innovation modules understand we're encouraging them to read in an interdisciplinary manner and they're routinely challenged with open-ended tasks to explore and reflect and connect their insights. Some of the PhD students we meet more briefly are simply challenged to think about how their research will be translated or made impactful for different 'real-world' audiences.

My Ideal Graduate

An ideal graduate will need to be able to recognise, or create, evaluate, and develop opportunities for creating value, for themselves and others, dependent on both their own view of satisfaction and enriching the ecosystem around them such that they will be supported if they stumble (if they just satisfy themselves, they may find themselves isolated). Having worked in and around the competency and employability agenda for approaching 20 years I think that means they need the skills required in that era and the ability to re-skill in readiness for the next one. Skills needs change over time, especially in terms of the 'hard' technical skills, for example coding languages. However, whilst the 'soft' skills do shift they have been more stable; collaboration skills, problem-solving, and presentation skills are perennials. Creativity, interest-ingly, seems to be shifting from a niche skill to a fundamental one as our circumstances change ever faster.

However, skills are the 'software' that runs on the system, we can always update and develop our skills. The 'hardware' that underpins our ability to deliver those skills in a regular and consistent manner is now something I regard as being of greater importance and more important to build early through education. This might be characterised by an individual's curiosity, confidence, ambition, resilience, self-efficacy, emotional intelligence, and self-awareness. If you are not motivated or interested, it is hard to use your skills to their best ability; if you are not self-aware of yourself or genuinely interested in building relationships with others you will not best judge how to use your skills to their greatest impact on your own or others' success.

I really like Roy Heath's[1] notion of the 'Reasonable Adventurer' and Colin Jones's work exploring that model.[2] A graduate possessing those six character-istics (Intellectuality, Close Friendships, Independence in Value Judgements, Tolerance of Ambiguity, Breadth of Interest, and Humour) comes as close as I have been able to set out the 'hardware' requirements of an ideal graduate.

Why this Type of Graduate?

In this fast-changing era two characteristics strike me as non-negotiable; the ability to both adapt and re-skill for those changing circumstances, and to possess sufficient self-identity (self-awareness, self-efficacy, and self-confidence) to stay resilient and grounded in the teeth of so much change and re-invention. Students need both an agility to move with the times, and also to be securely anchored to their own identity such that they do not feel un-tethered and lost from their moorings as they shift jobs, careers, locations, and roles. What creates, or reveals, their identity is what piques their curiosity and what they seem compelled to create when left to their own devices. If 'culture is what people do when no-one is looking' then identity is what students discover when they are not being instructed.

To deliver against both of these characteristics, students need to experience ambiguity and change; to work out which bits of their identities are more fixed, and which can shift. In complex and chaotic situations, it is next to impossible to try and impose a rigid pattern of rule-based action; it is far better to hold onto some principles and improvise as best you can around them. Adversity tends to break rigid brittle things and it tempers those things that can flex. A student who can undertake the necessary adventures of life in a reasonable (rather than a reckless) manner is far more likely to be able to find and exploit opportunities successfully and sustainably.

My Theories of Development

I have mentioned the work of Heath and Jones on the concept of the Reasonable Adventurer. I would then connect that work with Sarasvathy's[3] work on Effectual Logic as central to a body of theory in which attitude and outlook are critical elements in acting in ambiguous circumstances. I would also cite the work of popular writers on innovation such as Tim Harford,[4] Steven Johnson,[5] and Matthew Syed[6] for making an 'ecosystem' view of how creativity, innovation, and entrepreneurship occur both accessible and engaging (there is no substitute for a good story to illuminate an idea). I have increasingly dabbled in elements of systems thinking to deepen this ecosystem view without resorting to the original texts, but the work of professional practitioners and organisations like the Ellen MacArthur Foundation I find inspiring.

DEVELOPING ENTERPRISING CREATIVE THINKERS

As previously identified, I draw heavily on experiential learning methods to support the development of graduates' creative thinking. This is typically some form of problem-based learning format. Depending on the time available this might be one or two multi-week projects usually in the format of a challenge briefed by or for a real or imagined stakeholder, or an entrepreneurial venture-creation project, or, in the case of one first-year undergraduate unit, a series of one- and two-week challenges to explore, research, make, or respond to some small provocation (for example: run a team-building event for your group, complete a Personal Business Model Canvas, write a case-study analysis of one piece of marketing material).

These projects are typically supported by a front-loaded 'tools and methods for innovation'-based curriculum (i.e., a teaching-heavy start with some degree of 'flipped classroom' content that gives way to students simply working in groups with staff available for support). That curriculum typically introduces or refreshes the key tools and methods to be used; typically, a mix of human-centred design-thinking (to best identify and validate the need), value proposition design (to frame and hone the solution), and lean start-up (to work through rapid iterations of the solution and arrive at some impact).

'Core' study materials are framed alongside a wider body of sources (academic and professional papers, podcasts, news articles, books, exemplar case studies and so on) which are positioned as 'bonus material' or 'recommended reading' alongside my regular prompts to enrich their diet. There will always be a handful of repeated metaphors or motifs that loop through the material to provide a theme; usually concerning the value of failing fast, or learning to work with ambiguity, or to cultivate serendipity.

Alongside the project deliverable there is usually some form of parallel assessment activity; typically, a reflection, but often both a critical appraisal of some methodology used *and* a reflection upon its use. In the 'biggest' unit of this variety that I have developed we not only have students working in project teams on venture creation but also sitting on the advisory board of another team to gain a wider perspective.

Stages of Development

The stages my learners (and their ideas) go through are built around a design-thinking-informed process moving from highly speculative hunches to validated proposals. The students' learning follows suit through the experiential practice of speculating, researching, testing, failing, and learning.

Where they start from in the process really depends on the context of the unit. I sometimes teach students who have come into the unit with a robust idea that is ready to explore; we do sometimes get the chance to suggest and support students prior to the unit to bring some potential ideas, but often we must initiate this process of finding something worth exploring in the first class. As a result, the first stage of development is typically one of Exploration and searching for an idea (either in response to a brief or to an open venture-creation opportunity). Where a student starts with an apparently robust idea we will try to 'blow it up' by going back to the initial problem to prove it works and establish there are not better alternative approaches.

The second stage is one of Synthesis and Validation of the opportunity; can the students bring their search results back and go through that sense-making process to prove that there is something worth doing that looks desirable, feasible, and viable. Only then do we move into an Ideation phase of generating potential solutions and then Prototyping and Testing before Delivering. In the early years of our programmes and often in the context of short form teaching where I only have a single session to share this model, I would present this as a linear staged model, but for students who have some familiarity with the process we adopt a more Agile process with regular sprints and iterative loops through these stages.

Evaluating Outcomes

My learning outcomes, and the assessment formats that derive from them, focus on competency and criticality in using the methods and processes we teach. Assessments tend to be split between an 'authentic output' such as a *Report* or *Proposal* (either a venture plan, client report, and/or a presentation version of the same) in an appropriate professional format, some form of *Design Document* which provides a 'backstage' account of the methods and processes used to arrive at the Proposal, and a *Reflection* which demonstrates their personal and professional learning along the route. These elements are usually weighted equally within the assessment.

Whilst I believe that the Design Document and Reflection are the most important elements for demonstrating the learning that took place, I find that the Report or Proposal is the bit that students find useful to show others and put in their professional portfolio, as such it has value beyond the academic assessment and helps hone professional standards of presenting information that is workplace relevant (when done well and with reference to current and emerging professional practice).

The criteria used to then assess include some traditional elements like clarity of presentation, criticality of analysis, robustness of evidence, but I also ask for diversity of sources and methods and reward moving beyond the methods used in class. I tell my students that we do not assess the idea itself, only the process that they identified and the way they executed it. I similarly stress that I try to assess the 'distance and divergence travelled' considering the complexity of what was done and the resources the individual or group had.

Areas of Student/Graduate Difficulty

The first difficulty I typically encounter concerns attitudes to ambiguity. Some students find these open challenges and problem-solving briefs exciting and revel in the licence to explore, but equally some students resent not having a clearly defined objective or set of tasks to work to and struggle with the ambiguous and uncertain framing of what a good outcome or an ideal process might look like despite these being highly contextual when you compare founding a fast-food van business with a MedTech start-up. I try to assist them by variously breaking down the process into more manageable steps with recommended outputs for each step, or criteria to work to. Examples can be helpful, but I always try to present divergent options so that students do not seize on template answers. Voices from the real world that confirm the need to work with ambiguity also help students feel that this is not just an arbitrary academic decision.

Some groups struggle to get beyond the more obvious or common-sense solutions to more innovative solutions. This might reflect a lack of confidence, either in the process, or in potentially being radical or silly in front of their peers. Sometimes groups simply try to 'solve it' too quickly. To resolve this, I will run practices of the process and show examples of where 'silly' was a stepping-stone to something brilliant but unorthodox. I often force groups to maintain multiple answers for far longer than they would want to before settling on 'the idea'. Helping build the team through a discussion of personality differences, roles, and team-bonding activity is also a worthwhile investment to give them resilience in the process.

Alternatively, some groups struggle to constrain their creativity and resist finding focus and put off the process of testing and validating their ideas. On some occasions this is a reluctance to potentially debunk their own ideas and sometimes this is simply because they enjoy ideation and find the validation something of a graft. Again, a staged process, often with a formative 'scorecard' type self-, academic or peer-evaluation can help draw individuals and groups back to some sort of evaluative step at regular intervals without seeming too onerous.

My Challenges

In developing these approaches, the challenge is always trying to find the right balance of both structure and licence to explore, in the context of who the students are, how much time we have, and what the system permits us to do. However, what has been more revealing is the work I have done with other academics to embed this approach in *their* teaching. Whilst almost all have quickly embraced the value of an experiential and problem-based approach, you often must reassure them that they can release their grip on 'teaching content' and closely structuring both teaching and assessment, whilst creating a new supporting framework for enabling the students to learn. It means moving from teaching to facilitating, and that requires a different skill set, which in turn requires confidence to hold the whole thing together.

One further challenge has been resolving the problem of research ethics approval for students working in this way; how can you get formal ethics approval for students when you are trying to both work in an agile manner and not make all the work about how to write an ethics proposal. Students want to work on problematic issues like homelessness, mental health, and inequality which can make this very difficult.

Nature of Confirmation

Anecdotally I can point to a lot of students whose careers, self-confidence and application of tools would suggest that this approach has worked. This is true of both short workshops and whole programmes of teaching. A lot of students have informally and formally offered testimony that they have gained in entrepreneurial competence and creative confidence because of my teaching and of the teaching innovations I have supported in others.

Hard data that measures graduate success does exist, but it is harder to ascribe particular responsibility to my input, likewise I've not seen any metrics that prove my graduates have greater confidence in their creative abilities. I have picked up individual and team awards for my teaching at institutional and national levels but again we might debate what this 'proves'. Here is a little testimony from one student on our four-week online Innovation and Enterprise course:

> This course has helped me change my mindset from 'failure = give up' to 'failure = modify'. Seeing failure as a feedback rather than as the end of the road is very inspiring, and I believe will make all the difference in my future. Also, learning that anyone can be an innovator has moved me to see my ideas as innovations rather than just projects, because they all want to focus on enacting change and 'innovating' how people think by raising awareness. The thought that we have the power to engineer our luck was comforting, as it means we are in control of how we develop our ideas to take them to where we want them. On the other hand, we must also be accepting there are factors we don't control and see them as opportunities rather than setbacks.

SHARED WISDOM

The diet and exercise approach can obviously be applied widely; students in any discipline benefit from diverse and stimulating inputs that give them the raw materials to work with, likewise they would also benefit from a supported programme of being stretched towards goals that might initially seem intimidating. What I believe is less common is a teaching structure within which students are challenged to develop their own practice and work towards their own outputs; it is the development of their confidence to be creative, autonomous, and responsible for the value that emerges that enables them to be enterprising in the longer term.

I would encourage educators in all disciplines to loosen the shackles of what needs to be taught and enable students to find the possibilities of what might be learnt. Help students connect the taught material to the past, present, and future experiences of themselves and others and you'll empower them to be confident creatives able to work with ambiguity and create their own value.

My Development

In the words of Robert Poynton[7] 'Notice more, let go, use everything'; widen the lens when you teach and try to spot the connections and patterns, however tenuous or obscure, let go of rigid control and focus on building a secure framework within which students can explore for themselves, and be willing to use everything that emerges. It's taken me a long time to ween myself away from rigid plans towards a more improvised approach; I'm not winging it, but I've tried to create space in my classrooms to let the students mentor me more often than I used to.

By widening the lens of what my teaching is about (i.e., entrepreneurship as a process or method that has application and insight into almost any domain of knowledge) I find I can make more connections, I find I can help my students find relevance and use for their learning in their own lives, and more broadly I create more serendipity and more luck for all involved.

Lessons Learned

It has taken me 15 years to move from trying to find the 'right' answer to 'finding as many answers as possible' to 'finding the most divergent and interesting answers possible'. I would hope that others can make that transit quicker than I did. I'd also encourage other facilitators to enrich their own 'scrapyards of spare parts' that they can bring in to enrich their teaching; I'm persistently delighted by the way in which my brain draws upon divergent and apparently disconnected elements of my own experience to build new insights; it's almost as if I'm creating my own personal mythos.

NOTES

1.   See Heath (1964).
2.   See Jones (2011, 2019).
3.   See Sarasvathy (2008).
4.   See Harford (2016, 2017).
5.   See Johnson (2010: vii).
6.   See Syed (2019).
7.   See Poynton (2013: 15).

9.   Creativity as expansive learning

Daniele Morselli

In Change Laboratories the practitioners, sometimes also including students, patients, or clients, take over the leading role in designing their future. The taking over is a crucial feature of a formative intervention. The very point is to generate the unexpected – learning what is not yet there.
(Engeström, 2015: xxxiv)

As an educational researcher, my interest in creativity comes from the need to offer novel solutions to cogent problems in educational settings. In 2007 I spent two years in Israel working with special needs learners to develop their critical thinking skills through the Feuerstein methods. There I learnt the importance of mediation, that is a quality of human relationship that fosters human cognitive modifiability. During my PhD I was influenced by Cultural Historical Activity Theory (CHAT) and the importance given to dialectics and remediation to find collective and creative solutions to historically developing problems affecting organizations. My PhD work devises a model of sociocultural workshop for enterprise education. In it, vocational students undertaking work experience discuss the problems that the participation in two different activity systems (school and work) imply and find solutions that are then implemented. During my post-doc I used the Change Laboratory, a toolkit for innovation and social practices, for entrepreneurship education. Vocational teachers discuss the problems affecting their course, comprising the dramatic fall of new enrolment students, dig into the problems to find the roots of their problem, and find solutions and implement them, thus innovating their didactics.

MY TEACHING / FACILITATION PHILOSOPHY

The sociocultural workshops described here build on the Vygotskian process of double stimulation. In an experiment Vygotsky gave a child a problem beyond her capacity, that is a first stimulus. What he frequently observed was that, when a neutral object was placed next to the child, the child would take it into the problematic situation to solve it. In doing so, such second stimulus was turned into a meaningful sign that mediated the solution.

Double stimulation can be used in collective problems solving, and it becomes more complicated and distributed in time. During the Change Laboratory sessions, the participants discuss issues in their organization and build a shared comprehension of the systematic view of the problem and its origins, that is a shared first stimulus. To do so, I present the participants with mirror materials, problematic aspects of their work practices which they discuss, and progressively they develop an understanding of the systematic causes of their problems. Subsequently, I present a second stimulus, that is an idea or a concept that can be utilized as a tool to better analyse and conceptualize the first stimulus.

However, this process of looking for a solution cannot be easily controlled by me, and the participants tend eventually to build their own second stimulus and solution to the problem. Therefore, not only is double stimulation an essential process for creativity and problem-solving, but it is also the basic mechanism for the genesis of human will. In other words, I am convinced that double stimulation supports entrepreneurship both as creativity, sense of initiative, and agency.

MY CONTEXT

During Change Laboratory interventions 15 to 20 participants (practitioners, students, or both) helped by me as a process facilitator meet on a weekly basis for 8 to 10 meetings for a couple of months plus follow-up. Each meeting lasts a couple of hours, during which the participants analyse their organization studied as an activity system in a setting that promotes intensive remediation of work activity. A period of observant participation precedes the sessions. during which I collect ethnographic materials to be used during the intervention. These are called 'mirror materials'. I make a careful selection of these field materials that I use during the sessions to trigger deep analysis, discussion and involvement. To make an example of a mirror material, during the sessions with vocational students, their teachers and work tutors I showed a clip of an interview with a work tutor I had done two days before. In that interview, the owner of a restaurant having a student undertaking work experience explained why he had to dismiss the student, who was among the students participating in the sessions. This promoted the discussion of what had gone wrong and what could be done to solve it.

My Ideal Graduate

I select the volunteering participants from a pilot unit or a compact group of people who desire to engage in a meaningful change effort. I negotiate the course and content of the intervention with the organization, and the participants eventually determine the form that the intervention will take. Hence, a key outcome of the Change Laboratory is their agency and initiative. A collective and transformative agency happens when they break away from the given frame of action and take the initiative to transform it. This stepwise process is characterized by six expressions of agency:

1. Criticize the existing organization and activity;
2. Resist the interventionist or the direction;
3. Propose new possibilities;
4. Envision novel model or patterns of activity;
5. Commit to change the activity with practical actions;
6. Take these consequential actions to transform the activity.

Why this Type of Graduate?

The Change Laboratory intervention encourages expansive learning, during which the participants learn a set of skills such as: to question the present practices or wisdom; to analyse their organization, to model a solution, and to test and implement it. Such 'turning an innovative idea into practice', which in expansive learning is a collective process, is the core of entrepreneurship as competence for lifelong learning.

Moreover, during this process participants develop their agency. According to the OECD (the Organisation for Economic Co-operation and Development), agency implies a responsibility in taking part in the world to influence circumstances, events, and people for the better. The Change Laboratory process fosters co-agency, that is mutually supportive and interactive relations that help learners to advance towards the goals that are of value for them. On one hand, the idea that learners should develop their agency is connected to lifelong learning and with the many professional or life changes they will have to deal with. On the other hand, by finding solutions to collective and cogent problems the learners create value for their community, and value creation (either cultural, social or financial) is an objective of entrepreneurship education.

My Theories of Development

My facilitation philosophy is rooted in Cultural Historical Activity Theory and seeks to encourage expansive learning with collectives. Expansive learning goes beyond the metaphors of learning as acquisition and learning as participation, since it focuses on communities as learners, on creation and transformation of culture, on hybridization and horizontal movements between organizations, and on the creation of new concepts. Expansive learning starts when individuals begin to question an accepted practice or common wisdom, and this change process progressively expands in the organization. This learning process can be understood as building and resolving the evolving contradictions that concern the activity system. The novel concept or practice generated during the expansive learning process is a vision with commitment and initiative from the participants, which can be hardly controlled by the researcher or the management. The participants 'learn something that is not yet there' meaning that they design a new concept and object for their collective activity and implement them.

DEVELOPING ENTERPRISING CREATIVE THINKERS

The Change Laboratory sessions are characterized by a set of 3x3 writing surfaces (such as flipcharts) that I use according to a vertical and a horizontal dimension. The horizontal dimension represents the level of abstraction of the analysis. On one side there are the materials representing the most concrete level with the *mirror materials*; these are field materials gathered by the researcher and dealing with recurring problems of the activity, thus promoting discussion, involvement, and reflection on work practices. Mirror materials can be interviews with customers, statistics or documents involving the organization, or a video representing critical moments of work activities. For the other side there is the *vision/model* surface, where the participants discuss possible models or concepts of their activity. At the beginning of the intervention, I propose models that help the participants systematically analyse their organization and maintain at the same time a holistic vision of it. The triangular model of activity, for example, helps them analyse the organization inwards and visualize important connections, for example between the community, the division of labour, the rules, the instruments, the object of the activity.

The same model also helps see the relation outwards between the activity and the other interacting organizations. Another possible model is the cycle of expansive learning that helps situate the historical moment the activity system is at and the corresponding learning actions. In the middle of the horizontal dimension there is the *ideas/tools* surface for cognitive tools helping in the process, for example flowcharts and schedules, diagrams and layout pictures of organizational structures, classifications of the responses to the interviews, templates and formulas to calculate costs, space for brain storming including role playing and simulations. Eventually, the vertical dimension of the surfaces represents movement in time, between *past*, *present*, and *future*. The analysis according to an historical perspective helps the participants understand the evolving contradiction pervading the elements of the activity system. Only by analysing what the organization used to be and what it is presently, can the participants envision the actual possibilities of development of the organization, that is, its collective zone of proximal development.

Stages of Development

Expansive learning happens through a sequence of learning actions, for each of which, the facilitator designs specific tasks that the participants undertake. All together the actions below form a cycle of expansive learning. The sequence below is ideal, and the participants could move back and forward in the cycle during the sessions. A variable is the participants' will: at the beginning the intervention is guided by me, so that I can provide the participants with tools and concepts for the analysis, however the lead is progressively taken by the participants, who suggest tasks, therefore learning actions to undertake, and they ultimately set the agenda. Hence, as process facilitator, I have to deal with the dialectics between, on the one hand, designing and proposing tasks to have the participants accomplish specific learning actions, and, on the other hand, to encourage the participants' manifestations of agency. The actions of expansive learning are:

1. Criticize, question, or even reject aspects of the existing wisdom or accepted practices.
2. Analyse the situation to find possible explanations and underlying mechanisms. There are two types of analysis backing each other. The first is the historical-genetic analysis, which aims to explain the present situation by tracing its roots in the past and its development. The second is the actual-empirical analysis. It seeks to explain the present situation by finding the systematic relationships between its internal contradictory elements.
3. Model the new solution. Starting from this systematic contradiction, the participants design a solution, a concept or new model of activity that tackle this contradiction in an innovative way. This model is made in a public form that can be observed and transmitted.
4. Examine the new model, operate, and experiment with it to fully catch its internal functioning, potentials, and limitations.
5. Implement the new model through its application in practice, enrichment, and extension.
6. Reflect on and evaluate the expansive learning process.
7. Consolidate the model into a stable practice and generalize (in the same organization or in a new context).

All together these learning actions compose the cycle of expansive learning.

Evaluating Outcomes

The Change Laboratory is an open-ended process, and therefore it is difficult to know what the outcome will be like; however, I evaluated the intervention against the agency that the participants developed during the process. I expect the participants' agency to switch from individualistic behaviour, resistance and critics to me or the management, to active participation, commitment to cooperate, and implementation of the new idea or concept.

Another element I use to evaluate a Change Laboratory intervention is the nature of the new concept and model developed and its generalization to other contexts. On one hand, I appraise the extent with which the new concept tackles the problems that were discussed and the extent of innovation and advancements that its implementation brought in the organization. On the other hand, I evaluate the novel concept or model against its power to generate new powerful concepts that can be applied to other contexts, that is its generativity. The first dimension of generativity is the continuation and development of this concept in the same site of the intervention, for example another class in a school or university. The second dimension of generativity stems from the adoption of the Change Laboratory method in other sites and cultural context within the same domain of activity, for example another faculty in the university or another course in the school. The third dimension concerns the appropriation of method, when subsequent interventions develop further the methods that have been generated in a specific Change Laboratory.

Areas of Student/Graduate Difficulty

To promote expansive learning, I have the participants look at their activity through its historical and concrete context, thus helping them break away from abstract generalizations and myths. This is difficult at the beginning, because the participants have an abstract conceptualization of their activity which is hard to break.

I find it also difficult to keep a balance between the participants' emotional involvement and a distance intellectual analysis. Mirror materials such as videorecording of work activities showing issues, or critics from the customers can be emotionally challenging to tackle. By way of contrast, the intellectual analysis alone with no emotional involvement makes the participants miss motivation to find a common solution. Good mirror materials are those which arouse emotional energy, which can cause a participant pointing out something apparently contradicting the common sense or the established plans, which triggers discussion and upset. The participants often invoke myths to neutralize a questioning observation, for example by moralizing and blaming people of misconducts and errors. Sometimes they argue that the mirror material is a rare exception or an unavoidable mistake, other times they accept the unpleasant remark and start analysing the present situation to better understand it.

My effort is to turn the emotional involvement into an intellectual analysis, and to guide the discussion into the analysis of the systematic causes of the challenging situation. Moreover, I try to keep the analysis at the activity level, thus discouraging moralizing and blaming individuals, which tend to stop the expansive learning process. To counter such blaming I remind how important the instruments and the other elements of an activity system (the object, community, rules, and division of labour) are to carry out a collective activity.

My Challenges

In my view the challenges of the Change Laboratory pertain its organization and negotiation. First, the intervention requires an extensive period of participant observation (at least a month or two) to gather the mirror materials and start formulating a working hypothesis. Observant participation will be useful also in between the session and after the session to collect further data and evidence. As such, I need to spend a lot of time in the organization selected for the intervention. In this regard, Change Laboratory interventions are sometimes led by a member of the organization who does a thesis supervised by an expert.

The second Challenge is the selection of the group of volunteers that will take part in the intervention. On one hand, rather than collecting scattered individuals, the intervention should involve a restricted group such as a unit in a big organization or a class in the school, so that they will be able to carry out change in their activity system. On the other hand, the intervention must be negotiated with the management in the objectives, commitment, and time. In an intervention I collected the teaching body of a secondary vocational course in surveying who was facing the dramatic drop of new enrolment students. At the beginning the participants were not so involved, but at the end of the process they were committed enough to implement the idea they had designed for two school years.

Nature of Confirmation

The nature of confirmation comes from the participants' involvement during the intervention, for example I see the increasing commitment of the participants in the discussion and design of the idea, as well as new participants joining in the change effort. Another confirmation is that the participants not only come to the sessions and participate actively, but they also commit to change, and when the moment comes, they strive to implement their concept or idea in practice. On top of that there is an extensive body of literature[1] indicating that the Change Laboratory interventions produce change with novel concepts and practices.

SHARED WISDOM

A Change Laboratory intervention is particularly suited when an organization faces a major or contradictory problem or a transformation, and no one knows what needs to be done or learnt. Boundary Crossing sessions are organized between partner organizations to face a common problem. Moreover, it is important that during the intervention a good working atmosphere is established. On the one hand it is important that the Change Laboratory is negotiated with the management and that the participants receive support during the change effort. On the other hand, during the sessions the participants should feel free to discuss the problems without feeling that there are interferences or pressure.

My Development

Through the facilitation of Change Laboratory interventions, I have improved my understanding of Cultural Historical Activity Theory, which is necessary to carry out the intervention. In this type of intervention, it is self-evident that the quality of mediating tools for double stimulation is essential, to reflect on work practices, analyse the organization, and find a solution or model. I also became aware of the importance in between the sessions of having a supervisor or colleagues to discuss the choices and materials to use during the sessions.

Lessons Learned

My primary suggestion is to peruse the books on the Change Laboratory suggested in the References section and to understand well CHAT, for example through a reading group, since there are plenty of concepts characteristic of activity theory which are not immediate to grasp and to master: for example, +activity system, artefact, contradiction, expansive learning. It is also useful to discuss the intervention with a supervisor.

NOTE

1.   See Virkkunen and Newnham (2013), Engeström (2015) and Morselli (2019).

10. Creating a climate for creativity in the entrepreneurial classroom

Stefania Romano and Charlotte Carey

> You can't use up creativity. The more you use, the more you have.
> (Maya Angelou in Ardito, 1982: 33)

We have been working together for the last six years; we met at the ISBE (Institute of Small Business and Entrepreneurship) conference in 2015 in Glasgow, UK. We just 'clicked' and started developing research projects together and then later Stefania joined Charlotte to co-chair the ISBE Creative Industries Entrepreneurship conference track. Both of us teach in the areas of Innovation, Entrepreneurship and Marketing within British business schools.

This chapter is the result of an ongoing conversation and reflections between the authors. Using an auto-ethnographic approach we captured, in a series of semi-structured interviews between each other, over a period of two months the insights from this approach.

We have discovered something we have in common, through writing this chapter: we both started out in academia as researchers (following careers outside of the sector) and neither of us planned to become educators. It was for both by 'chance'. In addition, we both had a bad educational experience in tertiary education:

> SR: I hated school! it was boring, it was standardised, and it was no fun. However, I loved technical drawing and English (as a foreign language). I loved my English classes, my teacher used to talk about London, and I used to imagine the architecture (compared to Italy). I went on to study business but eventually did my PhD about creative industries.
> CC: My school experience was equally bad. I didn't seem to be academic, struggled with academic subjects, I loved Art and History I used to bunk off a lot, I was always called a daydreamer. Having left school at 15 I went to art school and following a number of general art and design courses I did a fine art degree and eventually (after a number of years working as a freelancer) a PhD about entrepreneurship within fine art careers.

We both felt we were not academically able. Nevertheless, both did well in arts subjects. As the quotes above suggest we were both considered 'daydreamers' and 'imaginers'. Ironically both are now acknowledged as essential drivers for the creative process.

OUR TEACHING/FACILITATION PHILOSOPHY

We have realised that as well as a similar educational experience, our teaching philosophies are closely aligned for example: to facilitate the diversity of learning styles and encourage active participation of students and to build confidence and acknowledge and identify the breadth of where creativity lies. How you get there is through experience, experimentation, and play.

> CC: I'm not sure it's a philosophy but it's an approach and that's experiential learning, learning by doing, and informed by creative discipline education. I've always felt we should teach business in art schools and not to art students I mean that we should use the setting and approach of an art school to teach business. I really benefitted from an art school education and the pedagogical approach I believe it lends itself well to many disciplines.
>
> SR: That's a humanistic approach and that's my philosophy it's 'freedom to learn' and experiential learning is the approach.

Humanism is based on the belief that individuals are free to learn and make their own decisions. In this context, the role of the educator is to facilitate the individual's discovery of relevant subject matter. For example, Montessori and Summerhill schools (launched at the start of the 20th century) believed in shifting the emphasis from teacher-centred to student-centred learning.[1] While these have been largely ignored by mainstream education in recent years, our sense is that they are being rediscovered by educators and have good fit for transformational learning, particularly given the diversity of the student body.

OUR CONTEXT

We are both working in Higher Education in Business Schools in the UK teaching at undergraduate, postgraduate, postgraduate research, and corporate level. CC teaches in a 'post 92' (an ex-polytechnic) which takes a very applied approach across all disciplines. SR previously worked in a similar type of institution and now works in a higher ranking and more research-focused institution. In our conversation, we talked about our observations of the two types of universities and that the newer universities tend to offer greater freedom and space for more creative teaching approaches.

> SR: Even though the context of where I am working (in a very research-orientated university) I still need colours, post-it notes, large paper and Lego! I bring the tools to enable students to experience creativity and to signal that this is a creative space. In my old university I used to throw balls around to ask students to

give examples – it was a game, who had the ball had to speak. Now that we're working online, I ask them to draw, to use Padlet (an online tool to make and share content).

CC: I try to create a real-lived experience through simulation/rehearsal, responding to live briefs, group work, drawing upon design approaches and design thinking. Based on my own education there's a lot about the way art and design is taught that helps students more broadly. Bringing in live clients and doing design tasks to hone ideas and then presenting (pitching) them to peers and lecturers works well in many disciplines and potentially leads to more enterprising behaviours.

Our Ideal Graduate

The type of graduate we develop, in terms of knowledge, skills and overall capability would have the following attributes: ethical, enterprising, a self-starter, curious, a problem-solver/solution finder, adaptable, confident but not arrogant, community-orientated, motivated, self-aware, kind/compassionate, generous, passionate and with an open and global mindset. Ultimately creative. These are all attributes, which arguably lead to a more satisfying career. That is not to say just financially rewarding but ethically, emotionally, and wellbeing-focused on a personal, community and global level. Arguably, this is fundamental for building responsible futures.

Why this Type of Graduate?

We are living in dynamic and challenging times but also a time of huge social change and potential opportunity. There is no one formula, way to do things, or individual that can solve these challenges or re-shape the historical legacy of how communities have been built, businesses and industries run. Graduates need to be in a position to actively be part of the change without being scared or overwhelmed to participate in the process. Our students are already technologically skilled, and our role is to nurture their talent, draw out and value their creative and design skills, harness their potential and passion so that they can contribute to positive societal and economic change.

When we look to the likes of Steve Jobs as an iconic design-led entrepreneur, Maria Montessori for her work in educational transformation, Maya Angelou for her contribution to writing, poetry and politics or Sir Ken Robinson for articulating the real and vital contribution of the arts, we see examples of individuals whose work has had a profound impact on the world. Their wisdom is arguably underpinned by shifting their negative experience, of the existing education system, into creative approaches, that then shape new visions for the world. We want to instil the confidence in our graduates that might lead them to believe they are able to embrace change and be the change like those iconic role-models. Universities, their culture, and environment have the opportunity to be the place of change for graduates to flourish. Arguably, traditional teaching practices hinder this.

Our Theories of Development

The theoretical basis for our approach could be described as: Transformational, Reflective and Contextualised. Within our teaching, critical thinking is highly encouraged during the workshops or the individual learning activities. In addition, an element of self-reflections, about experiences enables students to link the current situation to future job opportunities while empowering them with techniques to relate to others, via a transformative process and opening up new perspectives.[2] As Kolb[3] suggests "The central idea here is that learning and therefore knowing, requires both a grasp or figurative representation of experience and some transformation of that representation." Our interpretation of this is that when students enter the classroom, they bring with them existing experience and tacit knowledge. Through interacting with peers and educators, they create new meaning to these. What is more, our experience suggests that initially students are inclined to reject new ideas and so reflection is important to capture that transformation.

Within the field of entrepreneurship, considering context has become increasingly important.[4] The author's earlier research into Entrepreneurship Education suggested the need to consider context both in terms of discipline for example creative disciplines[5] and setting for example outside of HE within the community.[6] This has underpinned our approach.

Arguably, further contextualising and customising education enables us as educators to respect both introvert and extrovert learners (and the spectrum between) for example some might be 'observers' within the classroom setting and that's ok. Our approach includes all. It is a human-centred, design thinking approach insomuch that all stakeholders are considered. The classroom in this context becomes a space for co-creation of knowledge, where the students are not simply passive recipients of knowledge, but active participants.

DEVELOPING ENTERPRISING CREATIVE THINKERS

In terms of approaches and tools that we have deployed, for the most part we avoid the traditional 'chalk and talk' style of delivery. While there is an element of introducing topics, and the structure of the session, to orientate the students, the predominant approaches are: experiential learning through rehearsal and role-play; drawing, imagining and play. For example, using Lego bricks to create tangible scenarios or settings, to explore ideas.

A core aspect is borrowing from other disciplines. For example, theatre (improvisation and role-play), art and design (design thinking, experimentation, and pitch presentations). The experience of play and freedom is vital. We create a space for creativity within the classroom (particularly given the non-descript and often feature-less style of most university classroom settings). It is almost like the creation of temporary or 'pop-up' creative space.

In addition, some of the other tools we make use of within the classroom (and more recently through online delivery) are:

> SR: I use 'Padlet' to co-create. For example, to give students the opportunity to explore examples of different industries.

We both make use of case studies and entrepreneurial roles models:

> CC: Live case studies have been a really important feature and since working more online videos of interviews with entrepreneurs and creative thinkers. Particularly recent graduates working in our field as they're more relatable.
> SR: We also make use of well-established entrepreneurs who are 'Enterprise ambassadors'.
> CC: Social media and the internet as a space to rehearse and play has always been important to me, particularly for digital marketing and enterprise modules, and is especially gratifying when students professionalise and make businesses from their content creation.

This combination and variety of approaches offers students both the opportunity to explore their own ideas, see themselves as creative and also provides the context of the lived experience and how creativity manifests in entrepreneurship both on and off-line.

Stages of Development

Our learners go through various stages. Initially there is often some reluctance and resistance to the idea of participating in a creative-type session. Particularly if they are asked to do group work and if there is anxiety about the associated assessment. This might lead to them being stressed and sometimes mute, like they have a 'fight or flight' or in this instance mainly 'freeze' response. Of course, that will not be everyone and sometimes a more vocal student can be a real driver/role-model for others. Their experience and perception of creativity differs. For example:

> CC: I will often talk about creativity and there will be a range of responses and many 'I can't draw' – if I ask students to visualise or illustrate their ideas. I always say, "you can draw! You just stopped practising at some point in your

life and started thinking of yourself as not a creative person." So, there is work to be done in educating on what we mean by creativity and the breadth of it.

To reduce barriers to their resistance we acknowledge the different stages of their understanding. For example, as SR puts it:

> I put some Italian classical music on in the classroom. I want to give them this quality to connect with their hands, their heart, to stop thinking and turn-off the internal chatter – a sort of mindful activity.

Through a period of ideation divergent/convergent thinking and market research, students are required to apply design thinking and human-centred design approaches to problem-solving and ultimately find that they have great and numerous ideas. Finally, there is a stage where they are encouraged to acknowledge, based on the evidence through the learning experience, their own creativity and increased confidence.

Evaluating Outcomes

In terms of evaluating outcomes formative feedback and peer-reviewed feedback is ongoing. There are some benefits to working online. For example, using tools like Padlet, you can anonymise the students and they can peer-review each other's work and ideas and benefit from seeing all the feedback for all the students. We both recognise the value of summative assessment in the learning process:

> CC: I've always borrowed from art and design disciplines in assessing ideas. I went to art school where one's ideas were always assessed and so I feel like that's ingrained in how I assess. Partially it's about assessing their approach, and their rejection and development of ideas.[7]
>
> SR: In class verbal feedback is given to individual students to improve their writing, and articulation of ideas, to then provide them a structure or framework to present the utility of their ideas to different audiences. In addition, in their appendices I suggest they include all their creative processes.

Our Challenges

One of the issues over the years has been internal resistance of the institutions, or rigid thinking in terms of pedagogical approaches from departments or individual colleagues. Similarly, to Amabile[8] who identified the need to offer freedom to create. There is often a good intention to promote creativity but a misunderstanding of what it is, almost like creativity is pigeon-holed into art, music and so on, and viewed as something alternative or extra, as opposed to something that should be embedded into all our teaching and learning practices. These attitudes of both staff and students are no doubt amplified in the UK, by the current determination to promote STEM subjects across the education system and minimise the contribution of the creative discipline subjects.[9] This creates an atmosphere of belittling creative activities more widely.

From our perspective, as chairs of the ISBE Creative Industries Entrepreneurship track, this highlights a paradox within entrepreneurship/business education, which was explored through our work looking at the way in which creative industries entrepreneurship research is published.[10] In 2019 the creative industries in the UK (and pre-Covid-19), were the fastest growing sector in the UK, employing over 2 million people and contributing £13.5 million pounds per hour to UK Gross Value Added (GVA)[11] suggesting that creativity and creative pedagogies offer an economic and social value beyond the creative industries.

We have both been fortunate to be able to overcome some of the internal resistance by demonstrating student satisfaction, interest and subsequent module and dissertation topic choices. What has been really rewarding over the years is to follow the careers of alumni via social media, for example LinkedIn, and have them acknowledge the impact of their learning (and our creative methods) on their careers. This evidence base is powerful in making a case for more creative approaches.

SHARED WISDOM

We would like to share with other educators what we have learned so far:

> CC: I've always believed that creative and enterprising methods can be adapted to deliver teaching across any discipline. That how you teach has a bearing on creative and enterprising behaviours, in terms of how students solve problems and potentially leads to more entrepreneurial/intrapreneurial graduates.
>
> SR: I always want to cultivate intellectual and collective curiosity. The movement from an individual to collective thinking. It is like a dance. As the educator, you're the choreographer. I really believe that the classroom is a duplication of the real-world. We can give them the instruments and techniques to practise the challenges of working with the self, with others, to identify and balance individual skills and those of others and let the music play.

Our Development

Reflection has been vital in remaining flexible and adaptable. We might have developed approaches that we feel enable creativity to flourish amongst a diversity of students and cannot assume that what works for one year, one week, one group will still fit the next. Our experience suggests remaining open to your own ability to innovate, experiment and learn through unexpected sources provides you with the tools and techniques and confidence to evolve.

We should be like children, with an open mindset to explore learning in a versatile and organic way allowing the students to shape the learning environment and us to learn from them too.

> SR: For example, the other day the students left this message in the chatbox of a remote learning session when my internet connection was intermittent, they said: "Robot Stefania. Leave the session and come back." What I learned from them was to relax, have fun and to work with the unexpected and the unexpected but kindly nature of the student's communication.

Lessons Learned

Experiment, embrace your failures and be open to learn. Not everything will work immediately, but that does not mean you should play it safe. Sometimes we try something new. If it does not quite work out there is a danger that you revert to those existing, more traditional methods (e.g., read a paper and discuss in the seminar…). It might be that the timing is not quite right, the students are not ready, or they may be resistant, particularly if they cannot see the relevance of the session to the assessment. We have found being understanding, flexible, ready to adapt approaches and able to clarify the link to their summative assessment helps.

Evidence matters. Having evidence helps when making the case for your approaches to institutional management. For example: student emails (e.g., when they write to acknowledge that your module was the catalyst for getting a job or placement), sign-up for future modules, dissertation topics and ultimately graduate outcomes.

Be reflective and write about your practice. Being a reflective practitioner[12] enables an educator to develop a variety of approaches. According to the learning environment, styles and needs of the students, educators can be selective in choosing the most appropriate methods. Capturing reflections is important for the educator's development, shared institutional wisdom and beyond.

Finally, what if you experiment with your approaches? What if you embrace your own creativity, talent and bring your uniqueness to the learning environment? What you discover might be just be invaluable, after all, as Maya Angelou[13] stated, "you can't use up creativity. The more you use, the more you have."

NOTES

1.   See Bates (2019).
2.   See Christie et al. (2015) and Mezirow (2009).
3.   See Kolb (1983: 42).
4.   See Welter et al. (2019).
5.   See Carey and Naudin (2006) and Carey and Matlay (2011).
6.   See Hussain and Carey (2019).
7.   See Carey and Matlay (2010).
8.   See Amabile (1998).
9.   See Last (2017).
10.   See Carey et al. (2017) and Romano and Carey (2018).
11.   See the Creative Industries Council (2020).
12.   See Kolb (1983).
13.   This quote is attributed to Maya Angelou, from an interview she gave to Mary Ardito for the *Bell Telephone Magazine* in 1982.

11. Learning with a pencil, not a pen

Andy Penaluna

Big flashy things have my name written all over them. Well … not yet, give me time
and a crayon.
(Smith et al., 2010: 6m40s)

Despite earlier success, I wasn't doing so well with education by my mid-teens and my examination grades were very mixed as I wasn't seeing their relevance. Luckily, I discovered the challenge of mixing engineering and art as a technical illustrator and joined the ranks of visual communicators who drew amazing cutaway drawings and ghosted views, often of things that didn't exist, but were being imagined. Thus, an ability to visualise futures and communicate to others drove me, and I was taught through mentored experience, rarely through lectures. Theory usually informed progress, it didn't lead it.

A key feature of my learning experience was developing an ability to research beyond a single discipline, and to learn from others wherever I could. A designer creates many 'scamps' of an idea based on these insights; they are rough and readily disposable, leading to 'roughs', which are better formed. A set of roughs inform 'visuals', which are minimum viable products, not one, but many, from which a final solution can be drawn. The approach develops flexibility and adaptability in a way that can be evaluated by an educator, and I found it fascinating to watch as learners developed.

MY TEACHING/FACILITATION PHILOSOPHY

This is learning with a pencil and not a pen, because we can sketch out, rub out and revisit anything we accomplish. Seeing potential futures, mixing and matching knowledge with observations and insights leads to creative surprises, which underpins all I do. I watch, listen and learn, then connect, interpret and communicate. I believe that knowledge retaining should play second fiddle to being an able knowledge harvester, because creative people are curious, always interested in alternative views, spotting patterns, and seeing connections that many others have missed. Through this, they can adapt and change quickly when a situation demands it. Hence my teaching is less about telling, and more about helping to develop better questions that may lead us to new answers. Typified by the question 'why do we always do it that way?', my learners and I tread new paths and discover new possibilities together.

If your educator knows the precise answer expected, they can set you on a path to implement what needs to be done and in what order. Conversely, if the answer is as yet unknown, many 'correct' answers can be devised. So, if I were to teach theory first, I'd have already limited the thinking pathway. However, when I and my students attempt to respond to questions, we can draw upon theory that may or may not fit as we travel together on a learning journey. This is the realm of innovation not implementation.[1]

MY CONTEXT

I came to realise that I was often teaching my business clients as well as my design students, and common themes were emerging. By the early 2000s my alumni were telling me that business and creativity were the core aspects of advertising design, using persuasive communication in business contexts. By 2005 and through the intervention of my former bank manager wife Kath, I came to realise that entrepreneurial education was seeking the very things we already did, and that the competencies that we were already familiar with developing were now being called for in her domain. Like many other creatives the word entrepreneurship simply didn't sit comfortably with me, but she saw the alignment, drew me into MBA education and in partnership, put together what she was learning from design education into a series of papers.

Awards from the Higher Education Academy (now AdvanceHE) and an International Best Empirical Paper in Brazil persuaded me that Kath had a point, and within two years I found myself teaching other educators and engaging in policy making. Enterprise Educators UK elected me to be their Chair in 2011, and by 2012 the first QAA Guidance[2] kicked off a whole new adventure.

My Ideal Graduate

My new adventure, with the support of 32 country experts and the UN[3] and EU[4] led me to set up the International Institute for Creative Entrepreneurial Development (IICED) at University of Wales Trinity Saint David, so I will borrow from some of their observations.

First and foremost, and to mimic design education, we wanted our students to move from dependency on the educator to autonomy of thinking and action. This applied in teacher training as well as undergraduates, and extended to international contracts such as the seven-country South East Europe Centre for Entrepreneurial Learning's work on developing entrepreneurial schools. We specifically aimed to enhance flexibility and adaptability through creative thought generation. Educating the educators now includes Doctoral-level studies,[5] which draw on the EntreComp Framework[6] that we helped to develop.

The EU's OvEnt Study[7] identified that we were amongst the strongest in terms of attitude and skills development, and very highly ranked in terms of knowledge. Specifically, recurring competencies include autonomy, teamwork and collaboration, communication, and sense of responsibility. In addition, idea generation, organisation and management, taking the initiative, negotiation, and decision-making were recognised within our approaches, especially when working in situations that were ambiguous and uncertain, requiring significant self-awareness and self-efficacy. Our projects also demonstrated engagement with ethics, financial literacy and the environment, especially when solving issues related to sustainability and social issues. Perhaps interestingly, the OvEnt Study also picked up how we had learned from the diversity of our offerings, which aligns well with our design-led intention to see multiple perspectives.

Why this Type of Graduate?

Multiple perspectives mean multiple alternatives in terms of ideas, and having many ideas supports the ability to shift and change as the situation demands. When things change, if you already have alternatives in your head, the problem of finding a new solution has already started. Moreover, they are your ideas, not ones borrowed from others, so are far more motivational in terms of ownership.

When you can think wider and not just deeper, you have a greater resource to call upon, so observational abilities can extend a student's opportunities; they see the things that others may have missed. There is an increasing literature that tells us that new innovations sit at the boundaries of disciplines, not at their core, and I suspect that this is one reason why design education has never been overly precious about where inspiration comes from.

There is also an underlying problem for any creative, and that is simply that the newness should have an element of surprise. The more surprising, the more creative it is deemed to be. This, in turn, means that to communicate your idea effectively, you need to reflect in order to explain your own thinking strategies, for example how did the connection occur in your mind and what triggered it? Why is it relevant to others? Why would it be of use in the future? This all sounds like getting better at pitching, doesn't it?

My Theories of Development

'Functional fixedness' is a term used to describe when things are done the same way, simply because they have always been done that way. 'Premature articulation' is when you jump to your first idea, but may not have developed potential alternatives to compare it to. In academia, we often place greater emphasis on criticality and being critical than being exploratory, but without good exploration, there is little new to critique! I often find myself discussing critical synthesis, and my contention is that we need more linking and connecting of disparate things. This ties in well with cognition research that tells us that our brains actually function differently when being critical and analytical to when we are being creative. Different areas of the brain are in use and different emotional situations can predetermine whether we use analytical (critical) thinking or insightful (pattern recognition / linking new thoughts) types of thinking.

DEVELOPING ENTERPRISING CREATIVE THINKERS

It is quite likely that when students first join us that the experience of examinations drives much of their thinking, and they have become used to recalling correct answers with no opportunity to challenge the questions being asked. Our first task is to break them away from this mentality by introducing progressively wicked problems to solve, ones where the answers cannot be certain, and where the argumentation for a solution takes priority over the outcome.

We also introduce scenario-based projects, where our students have to discover the problems in the context given before they can start to search out solutions. This searching out triggers investigative approaches that have to be carefully reflected upon to make sense to others, for example a hidden pattern may emerge that needs explaining before any potential solutions can be considered. Once the project is underway, these scenarios can be modified and changed, ideally because of something real and relevant that the students will believe is credible. Not only does this mimic the real world they will operate in, but it provides key points for mapping their ability to reflect, adapt and respond to change.

This approach not only helps them to come up with the multiple ideas discussed previously, but it also helps them to communicate when they increasingly become engaged in what we call 'live projects', when external needs and desires have to be addressed and the value of their thinking skills is put to the test through interactions with clients and customers.

Stages of Development

The 'master plan' is to enable students to develop so that they become:

*   Increasingly less dependent on the educator, and more independent thinkers and doers.

- Able to deal with increasing complexity and ambiguity and change.
- Consistently able to creative novel solutions within the stages of their learning journey.

The first stage is typically designed to wean students away from their schooling and the desire to please the educator by dispelling the notion of 'correct' answers for everything. This has the advantage of introducing the value of multiple stakeholder perspectives and quickly moves them from what the educator wants, to what the community and others may want. Using wicked problems as a vehicle to achieve this, theory is gradually introduced that supports their practical studio-based learning. Theory is rarely offered at the outset, as that will predetermine what they believe to be 'correct' and limit the divergent thinking and research-orientated abilities that we wish to develop.

The second stage takes this a step further but introduces more realistic scenarios within which to work. For example, alumni help to set projects based on their experience following graduation. External problems set by outside agencies and bodies are first reviewed and mapped against the learning level, then introduced into the learning at the appropriate juncture. Students are always encouraged to question what they are given, and not take it at face value.

Finally, students undertake two major 'capstone' projects or group of projects, which are negotiated following a pitch to the educator team. One (Personal Project) asks them to recognise their personal areas of weakness and requires them to design a project to address these, and the other (External Project) responds solely to the needs of an outside client. A self-funded group exhibition aimed at professional agencies and experts concludes the program.

Evaluating Outcomes

Although external views and opinions are used to gauge the effectiveness and novelty of posited solutions, for example through engagement with alumni and external partners, a considerable emphasis is placed on the students' ability to become better communicators when expressing how their solutions evolved. We look for well-evidenced research and well-considered argumentation, and wait to be persuaded that their ideas are appropriate, even if they are as yet unactionable.

The primary vehicle for this is the formative 'crit' or critique, an established methodology in the arts. This is not dissimilar to a pitch, but specifically engages the students when (a) a change has been introduced to their projects, and (b) when interim deadlines are set to review their multiple solutions. Within a crit students are set a minimum number of alternative solutions to discuss, and are asked to articulate how their thinking evolved, especially in terms of connecting things in new and different ways to ensure novelty. Their reflections are evidenced through a portfolio of developmental work that clearly articulates progression.[8]

Individual or group crits prepare students for a summative crit where their entire portfolio is presented. Contribution audits are used within group work to help to ensure fairness of evaluation. Perhaps worthy of note, is that their ability to do this improves dramatically following the first two or three audits, which are effectively discounted in assessment as they are merely learning aides. There are no examinations in the program.

Areas of Student/Graduate Difficulty

Initially students struggle with the concept of no correct answers, and ask naïve questions such as 'what do I have to do to get a first'. They also have difficulty when required to work in teams as the notion of fairness of grade is prevalent. Three approaches assist us to get past these issues quickly. First, by asking them to produce mini CVs and developing teams through engaging the right competencies helps them to move beyond their initial ideas of simply recruiting friends or people that they get along with. As the program evolves, they are given opportunities to hire and fire team members, and to give objective reasons behind the request. This is an example where emulating what actually happens in the creative industries works well and is supplemented by a powerful third approach.

The students increasingly engage with alumni who can evidence the value of the method and can contact them through regular online chats and presentations. A group question can be posted on social media for example, and alumni responses reviewed in the next class. This immediately ensures clarity in terms of relevance of their learning, and ensures that any questions to alumni are well considered before being asked. Having been helped this way, graduates are often keen to be the next supporter of learning and want to share their experiences, thus a continuous cycle of opportunity results.

My Challenges

Few challenges relate to student and alumni perspectives, but mostly to quality assurance and internal university validation procedures. For example, the introduction of new information part way through a project and the adjustment of interim deadlines was initially considered to be unfair to students. The employment of alumni in assessment was critiqued and in one particular instance, a course proposal was turned down because the argumentation for mixing design staff with business staff was considered too problematic in a course that was entirely new to the UK HE sector. It was approved one year later than planned, partly because another institution took the lead and developed a very similar program, and partly because at the second attempt nearly 300 alumni actively supported the proposal.

The experience of navigating these difficulties has been extremely useful and, for example in 2009–10, helped us to develop the UK's first formally validated teacher training for entrepreneurial educators. There are now many calls for more flexible, adaptable creative thinkers who can respond to the needs of others and create value through problem discovery and solution finding.

Nature of Confirmation

Without doubt, it has been the alumni support that has convinced me to keep progressing, especially when times have been difficult. The formalisation of bringing alumni perspectives into play was initiated in 1987–88 when two alumni fed back what they were learning on an entrepreneurship program with Professor David Kirby, and when others who had started up new business ventures simply wanted to say thank you. They all noted the alignment with their studies, and by 1996 our 'Continuous Conceptual Review Model' was accepted and used in new program validations. Later in 2005, and due in part to Professor Kirby inviting us to write for an entrepreneurship conference, we discovered kindred spirits, and received an award for Best International Empirical Paper at IntEnt 2006 in Brazil.

To fast forward to today, I now lead the UK Quality Assurance in Higher Education team on Enterprise and Entrepreneurship, and contributed to the development of the EU Joint Research Centre's EntreComp Framework. I have worked with the OECD and World Bank as well as the United Nations Conference on Trade and Development, where I supervised high-level international research. The science of Cognitive Neurology now clearly supports the teaching we developed.

SHARED WISDOM

I have come to realise how closely the role of design educators mirrors what enterprise and entrepreneurship educators are now attempting to achieve in terms of learning outcomes. This is in part confirmed by the emergence of design thinking as an approach, though as yet this to me feels like a thin veneer of what actually goes on within a design course. In terms of opportunity recognition, for example, I was fortunate enough to supervise PhD research in Ireland that confirmed the additional depth of thinking that developed in design when compared to business and management schools.[9]

Designers don't close their minds by only looking at the academic literature in their own discipline but are very open to the views of others and seek out alternative dialogues that enable them to see new perspectives. They are inherently interdisciplinary learners who often have to research their client and their working environment before starting to think about solutions to the problems and issues they are presented with. As Clair Guyton of Saatchi and Saatchi explained to my students, Monday was the Territorial Army, Tuesday was Metro-Goldwyn-Mayer films and Wednesday was Eukanuba dog food.

My Development

This could be a long answer, as I started my teaching career alongside my free-lance business in 1980. However, I taught what I had studied, in the manner that I was taught myself, which as it turns out proved useful. I recently had a discussion with my old tutors (we didn't call them lecturers) who confirmed that the intention then, in the late 70s, was the intention I have now – to help students to survive, then thrive, in a fast-moving interdisciplinary environment.

Undertaking a two-year teacher training program at the University of Wales in the early 80s made me start to dig deeper, and I became extremely interested in the psychology and emotional aspects of learning. What has improved subsequently is my theoretical engagement in all things related to learning and teaching, and although it can still be challenged, learning about the learning brain and how creative insightful thinking is significantly different to analytical thinking; it relies on critical synthesis as well as critical analysis. I find the ongoing research by Mark Jung-Beeman and John Kounios particularly intriguing, as it supports so much of how I intuitively taught, based on my own learning experiences. I can spot gaps too!

Lessons Learned

Well, the sharing with other educators has to be the main thing, but with an eye on what they are trying to achieve and where distinctions and differences may lie. I come from design, but called upon 32 different disciplinary approaches when presenting my first ideas on quality enhancement in enterprise and entrepreneurship. I commonly say things like 'if you want to think about competitiveness and performance, go ask a sport educator', or, 'If you want to get deep into persuasion skills go ask a performing arts teacher, because their students can convince you that they are someone else altogether.' When I was lucky enough to be elected to Chair Enterprise Educators UK in 2011–12, I was blown away by expertise in areas one might not naturally go and look.

When you want a quick answer, think A to B and fly down a motorway at speed, when you want to think creatively, meander down the back roads, cross water if you can, and have the clear intention to take in as much as you can on your journey. A small notebook and a few pencils or crayons will help to record emerging observations, thoughts and ideas. The more you become aware of what is in your mind, the more connections you can make in unusual and unique ways.

Just give yourself time and a crayon!

NOTES

1. See Penaluna and Penaluna (2015).
2. See QAA (2012).
3. See Mugione and Penaluna (2018).
4. See case studies 4 and 8 in Komarkova et al. (2015).
5. See case studies 7 and 9 in McCallum et al. (2018).
6. See Bacigalupo et al. (2016).
7. See Komarkova et al. (2015).
8. For a detailed discussion, see Penaluna and Penaluna (2020).
9. See Tynan (2017).

12. Entrepreneurial opportunities by design: unlocking creative potential

Margaret Tynan

> What we need is more people who specialise in the impossible.
> (Kizer in Roethke and Kizer, 2013: 93)

I come from a long line of educators, so as they say, education is in my blood. I studied and mastered in business, which is the lens through which I deliver enterprise and entrepreneurship (EE) education. My early life has shaped who I am. Throughout my youth, my father ran a part-time publishing business and as a rite of passage my family spent their formative years working there. Thus, my interest in entrepreneurship was born. My creative orientation comes from my mother, an incredible problem solver.

My academic journey as an EE educator began in 2001. However, my view of EE changed by participating in the International Entrepreneurship Educators Programme, hosted by the National Council for Graduate Entrepreneurship (NCGE) in 2010. This is where I first encountered the concept of the entrepreneurial mindset, and it opened my mind to a world of educational possibilities. This experience put me firmly on a new path which resulted in a complete re-think of my approach towards EE education.

MY TEACHING/FACILITATION PHILOSOPHY

My teaching philosophy attempts to ignite students' passion for entrepreneurship while nurturing their belief in their creative potential. I endeavour to tap into students' natural curiosity, allow them to explore and I encourage them to play with ideas before they develop those with potential.

Pittaway and Edwards[1] classify different types of EE education as: about, for and through. I am more firmly in the through camp where my focus is on learning through doing, in a safe environment. Action-based learning is well recognised in EE education circles as enabling entrepreneurial self-efficacy, facilitating the development of entrepreneurial behaviours, and developing key entrepreneurial skills, such as creativity.

There is a well-founded belief that entrepreneurship starts with an idea. Indeed, many entrepreneurship events start with a creativity or ideation exercise to flush out entrepreneurial ideas. But how often do people stop to think about where these ideas come from? How do entrepreneurs come up with those creative ideas?

In response to those questions my approach towards EE education has become design-informed. I was inspired by Andy and Kath Penaluna[2] who claimed that design educators do not expect their students to "blindly go looking for new ideas but train their students to employ a set of approaches that may lead to discovery", enabling them to respond to problems and see them as opportunities.

MY CONTEXT

While I deliver EE at all levels in Higher Education in Ireland, I relish engaging with first-year students most. These students emerge from an Irish second level education system, criticised for programming students to 'learn the right answer' through rote memorisation. The dominance of this thinking conditions students to believe that there is always a 'right' answer and that the educator will tell them what they need to know. I do not conform to this belief, but I recognise the damage confined thinking does to students' curiosity and creative self-efficacy. I try to open students' eyes to recognise the creative freedom offered through enterprise.

My focus in the early stages of undergraduate education is on the entrepreneurial mindset. Research indicates that creativity and opportunity recognition are the two most commonly mentioned competences in EE education, yet evidence suggests that there is little effort to develop them as competences in Higher Education environments. Therefore, I have designed my modules to introduce students to processes and ways of thinking that specifically focus on these competence areas.

My Ideal Graduate

I aspire to nurture confident, creative, resourceful, and resilient graduates who do not feel restricted by the current state of play. They relish a challenge and believe in their ability to make change happen. These graduates see possibilities where others see problems. They are driven by their curiosity to learn and to discover new things. They not only function in society but contribute to its evolution, powered by their entrepreneurial knowledge, skills, and capability.

These graduates have personalised what enterprise means to them and are self-directed in identifying opportunities that are right for them. They are grounded in the reality of what an entrepreneurial way of life involves and are excited by the prospect. They appreciate that each entrepreneurial journey is unique and that they must create their own path. They know how their specialist knowledge fits in this journey and recognise their strengths and limitations. They know they cannot embark on this journey alone, so they build a web of support around them to help achieve their goals.

Throughout their studies they have acquired skills that enable them to demonstrate entrepreneurial behaviours. They are creative thinkers who take time to assimilate knowledge, to understand problems, to empathise and to link un-associated pieces of information in ways which produce novel solutions to problems. They are skilled in opportunity recognition, recognising it as a process rather than an event. They are dreamers, as they are not afraid to wonder 'what if'. However, they are also pragmatists, embracing their ability to think rationally to distinguish between folly and feasibility.

These graduates know that they can create their own future. They don't accept the status quo and they know that they have the ability to do things differently. They look to the future and create opportunities to make things better for themselves and for others.

Why this Type of Graduate?

The ability to recognise opportunities to add value to their own, and others' lives, is considered essential in the face of globalisation and rapid change. Alan Gibb[3] argued strongly in support of the entrepreneurial mindset, to equip students to succeed in an increasingly global and turbulent world.

Change brings with it opportunities to do different things and do things differently. As EE educators we need to allow our students to be curious, to seek out relevant information and to have the confidence to experiment with ideas before they commit to developing them as entrepreneurial opportunities. Creativity and risk go hand in hand, so we must equip our students to be resilient and resourceful in responding to potential acclaim, criticism, or outright rejection. Creative mindsets do not work alone, and they need cues from others to help them understand, to let them know they are on the right track or to signal that further changes are needed.

Creative ideas are the feedstock for opportunity recognition which in turn allows graduates to create tomorrow's reality for themselves as individuals, for society and for economies. This view of opportunity recognition is informed by Baron[4] who defines it as the "cognitive process (or processes) through which individuals conclude that they have identified an opportunity". An opportunity, in this context, is defined by the author as: A chance to add value by doing something novel in response to a problem.

My Theories of Development

Again, I was influenced by the work of Andy and Kath Penaluna[5] who argued that the creative mindset required by EE education was little understood. As opportunity recognition is a creative process, I responded to calls from the design community[6] to consider pedagogies considered suitable for EE education. Rather than limiting myself to design thinking methodologies, I looked to the field of design education for inspiration.

Penaluna and associates[7] explain that pedagogic approaches used in the design disciplines tend to emphasise the process rather than the output. The literature suggests that design education delivery nurtures creativity, promotes critical thinking, reflection, and innovation.[8] My own research[9] subsequently demonstrated the potential to enhance opportunity recognition competence by incorporating creative approaches used in design education.

DEVELOPING ENTERPRISING CREATIVE THINKERS

The catalyst is a design brief, exposing students to wicked problems and presenting several constraints which must be accommodated in the final solution. Student *must* begin by understanding the problem. This stage of the process is not rushed, and I encourage students to take time to explore the problem space. The use of simple frameworks such as the five whys, fishbone diagrams, or a problem tree can help visualise their analysis.

Students are encouraged to empathise with those for whom they are solving the problem. The quality of this engagement is important, so they practise interview and observation techniques. Solution generation is encouraged once the problem is understood, albeit this can happen throughout the exploratory stage. Common creativity techniques can be helpful to flush out alternative ideas, combine ideas or to improve upon existing ideas. Students are urged to generate multiple solutions before narrowing their selection according to constraints outlined in the brief.

Peer sharing of information is key throughout the process where students pool their findings, identify gaps in their knowledge, share insights and provide feedback to each other. As the educator, my role is to challenge what they know, to get them to articulate their insights and ideas and to send them back for more, where needed.

Importantly, students must demonstrate *how* they arrived at their solutions and how their solutions relate to their *insight* of the problem. However, they must ensure that their solutions also meet the requirements of the brief. Both I and their peers offer feedback, providing students with the opportunity to reflect and revisit their solutions.

Solution selection requires students to evaluate their proposed solutions as potential business opportunities. They are encouraged to communicate their selected solution in a visible form as they re-engage with potential customers for feedback. Further modifications are made to their solutions where necessary. Finally, students must justify their final business opportunity to an assembled audience, illustrating how and why the solution has evolved to its final form.

Stages of Development

This process exposes students to all five stages of the opportunity recognition process:[10] preparation, incubation, insight, evaluation, and elaboration. Creativity needs time, so by design, the emphasis in early-stage undergraduate education (in terms of time allocation) is on opportunity recognition. This is reflected in the learning outcomes, allowing time to facilitate initial development of creativity competencies. In later years of EE, all five stages of the opportunity recognition process are still experienced, thereby reinforcing skill building. However, at this stage the emphasis deliberately shifts to creativity in the final two stages, in terms of depth of evaluation and exploration of options for opportunity elaboration.

The influence of design education approaches deliberately exposes students to all stages of the Double Diamond design process.[11] By encouraging students to explore a problem they must open their minds and 'go wide' into the problem space, learn to tease it out, learn to question and identify insights. These insights allow students to achieve a focus for solution development. Similarly, the process of generating solutions requires them to 'go wide' again and to generate many options. Using the brief, insights gained and given criteria, students must then filter and narrow their options once again. The final selection, based on opportunity evaluation criteria, is open to further exploration at the elaboration stage, until students determine the opportunity's final form.

Evaluating Outcomes

I have to admit to much experimentation in this area, reflecting developments in my thinking over time. My own research revealed that many EE educators are not comfortable assessing the creative aspects of EE, yet design educators have well-established, robust assessment strategies in this area.[12] I am influenced by Andy and Kath Penaluna's Design-Based Enterprise Assessment Model[13] as an approach to evaluate student performance.

My shift in focus, away from the product of opportunity recognition to the process, directed me towards learning portfolios as a method of formative assessment. These are frequently used in design education as they demonstrate engagement with the process in action. Students capture relevant sources of information, inspiration, thoughts, and conclusions from their research in addition to initial ideas, idea development, feedback and reflections. Portfolio assessment evaluates the range and depth of information gathered on the problem space, the application of frameworks and tools, evidence of empathy, evidence of idea generation and informed idea development. The final criteria are based on the depth of reflection throughout the process.

At a summative level, students are assessed based on their ability to verbalise their thinking. Students are required to orally present their knowledge of the problem space and visually demonstrate and defend their final solution to an assembled audience, at the end of the module.

Areas of Student/Graduate Difficulty

Requiring students to identify their own problem can be problematic. Indeed, starting with a 'blank sheet' is recognised as a barrier to creativity,[14] so students immediately hit their first hurdle. Scaffolding the process, by providing a problem brief, can help students engage. This brief, rather than being prescriptive, should present 'wicked' problems,[15] which provide multiple avenues from which to explore.

Starting the process can be challenging, after all we tackle wicked problems which cannot be solved by one simple solution. Students can initially feel somewhat lost in the problem space. They have so many possible avenues they could explore, and often they look to me to tell them the right one to follow. However, I push them to follow their curiosity, and ask them about the angle they are most interested in. I circulate between groups, answering their questions, discussing what they have found, asking them where they would like to go next, encouraging them, and assisting them, to use the frameworks and tools available to them.

Year on year I observe students demonstrate 'premature articulation'[16] where they rapidly identify 'the answer'. This can happen without the slightest insight into the problem. It is my role to challenge their thinking, send them back to explore and not to accept their first answer. I challenge them to look at things from different perspectives, to question what they accept as being, to observe and to discover insights. This provides the fertile bed for creativity to flourish.

My Challenges

When I began to look at this area, there were few practical resources available on opportunity recognition. Therefore, I practised as I preach, and I immersed myself in the area to truly understand it. Discovering the overlaps between opportunity recognition and creativity pulled me outside my comfort zone into an entirely different field.

I took a risk in translating what I had learned into practice. While I carefully crafted my module, and I understand *how* my approach enables the learning outcomes, I had to trust the process from the outset. I didn't know what students would discover, and I had to be ok with that. I could not control the material they would review, the people they would speak with, and I had no idea what types of solutions they would come up with. Ultimately, I had to relinquish control of aspects of student learning to the students themselves.

I quickly realised the importance of initial scaffolding. For early-stage undergraduates, scaffolding in terms of workshop structure, activities, times-cales and the use of frameworks is important as students are learning the rules of the game and loosening their 'one right answer' perspective. Such unlearning is considered necessary for creative thinking to take place.[17] For many students it is their first time negotiating this type of process, so these scaffolds are necessary to help them navigate their way.

Nature of Confirmation

Students don't always understand why we have to take a step back into the problem space before we can solve it. For me, the greatest demonstration of the efficacy of this approach is watching students divert away from their original assumptions about a problem and follow their curiosity to learn about some aspect of it they had not even considered before. Similarly, I see this approach working when students move away from their first idea to something more relevant. Students who truly engage in the process develop opportunities which reflect the depth of their engagement, and which clearly add value to others. Those 'eureka' moments still exist, when students identify a better, faster, or different way to provide their solution. I love nothing more than to hear and see the enthusiasm students have for their solution and their ability to sell it with passion.

I am not claiming that these behaviours are not evident using other approaches. The adrenaline rush that comes with creating a solution which appears truly exciting, is one of the best. However, using this approach students can appreciate *how* they have arrived at their solution and it provides them with the knowledge and creative skills to do so again.

SHARED WISDOM

The application of this approach is limitless. Design-informed creative thinking, leading to the identification of new opportunities, can be applied to a range of contexts such as individual, educational, societal, and commercial. I am mindful, however, of criticisms from Dorst,[18] Stewart[19] and others in the design community, regarding the growing popularity of Design Thinking. Much of this debate surrounds the positioning and perceived simplicity of the popular design thinking process and the manner of its use in other contexts. Critics suggest that in its current form it lacks depth, resulting in claims that design has so much more to offer. While there are overlaps in the stages of design thinking with my own approach, there are also important differences. Enabling 'designerly thinking' is not just taking people through a number of steps. Its success lies in understanding why it is done this way, how it is done effectively and understanding the vital role that the educator plays in enabling it. This is one area where design education has much to offer practitioners.

My Development

While I now understand how creativity and opportunity are closely intertwined, I also realise that my role as a facilitator is critical. While students engage with the process, I must enable them to perform. Many first-year students are afraid to voice their opinions and to articulate their ideas so the prospect of having to identify a business opportunity can be terrifying. It is my role to motivate, to reassure, to answer questions, to help, to encourage them to trust the process, trust each other and to trust me. I am critically aware that I need to create an environment in which students feel supported, where they can be creative, where they know its ok to fail at first and where their ideas won't be ridiculed.

I regularly work in workshop format, with students working independently together as I move between groups. As the educator, my knowledge of the process and how it enables creativity has changed my thinking, from seeing creativity as a 'topic' on the module to something which features throughout. Indeed, the European Commission[20] extolls the value of having creative educators with a good understanding of ways to integrate creative approaches into what they do, to enable creative learners.

Lessons Learned

Enabling creative thinking, while tackling wicked problems, broadens the scope for all students to arrive at novel solutions. It also helps students to realise that the potential for business opportunities is limitless. Working through this approach demonstrates to students that they have what it takes to solve complex problems and to do it in a meaningful way.

As we work with undergraduate students, we must appreciate that they do not always come equipped with the skills and the confidence to engage in creative activity. Therefore, we need to work with them to expose them to situations which will allow them to develop creative self-efficacy. We must also recognise that this happens, slowly, over time so therefore we must consider how we can provide opportunities for repeated exposure to creative processes in EE education.

When we encourage students to be creative, we too must understand what we are asking our students to do and how they can do it, so that we can support them in this endeavour. Speaking as someone whose entire academic experience is Business School oriented, we should not be limited by the blinkers of our discipline. We should reach out and look to the expertise of our colleagues in the creative disciplines to enhance our understanding of creative processes and enable us to become better educators.

NOTES

1. See Pittaway and Edwards (2012).
2. See Penaluna and Penaluna (2009: 729).
3. See Gibb (2007).
4. See Baron (2006: 107).
5. See Penaluna and Penaluna (2008, 2009).
6. See Penaluna et al. (2013) and Carey and Matlay (2010).
7. See Penaluna et al. (2013).
8. See European Commission (2009).
9. See Tynan (2017).
10. See Hansen, Lumpkin and Hills (2011).
11. See Design Council (2007).
12. See Carey and Matlay (2010).
13. See Penaluna and Penaluna (2009).
14. See Newton (2012).
15. See Dorst (2003).
16. See Penaluna et al. (2013).
17. See Penaluna, Penaluna and Diego (2014).
18. See Dorst (2011).
19. See Stewart (2011).
20. See European Commission (2009).

PART III

The ventures

13. Where the brave venture

Kath Penaluna

> Dear friend, theory is all grey, and the golden tree of life is green.
> (Allan and Kingdon, 2002: 93)

This final section takes us to the top of the QAA (2018) gateway triangle,[1] where discipline knowledge combines with enterprising skills to create the potential for venture creation. Policy recognition for entrepreneurship across the globe has been predominantly for its contribution to economic growth[2] for which education is seen as a vital driver, and perhaps in consequence entrepreneurial education is one of the fastest growing fields of education.[3] Graduate startups make a significant economic contribution and 'entrepreneurial eco-system' is the latest buzz phrase among those excited about the impact well-educated and entrepreneurial graduates can make to the country's financial outlook. According to the Higher Education Statistics Agency (HESA), in the UK alone almost 14,000 student startups and social enterprises generated £821 million in turnover in 2018.[4]

Yet, the contributors who have penned chapters in this section do not tend to reference economic contributions within their narrative as indicators of successes. Instead, they concentrate their discussions on the positive social impact entrepreneurship has on their graduates and their stakeholders. While Suntola (Chapter 18) acknowledges that entrepreneurship can be very financially profitable, she believes that for most, the motivation to build a startup is more heavily weighted towards making something meaningful. Kirby's (Chapter 16) ideal entrepreneurial graduate would be one that can bring about change and improvement to the world, with concerns for the environmental and social problems that profit-orientated business might bring. These are inspiring insights that have been offered in uncertain times, from those who interact closely with students. Of course, the idea of a healthier economy as a result of all this good work is also cheering when turning our gaze towards the future. The motivation and passion for doing good brings to mind the observation of Hamel,[5] that, "Passion is a significant multiplier of human effort, particularly when like-minded individuals converge around a worthy cause."

This notion of entrepreneurship being a vehicle with which to serve others positively is also reflected in the contributors' experiences of developing their current approaches. It is striking how much the facilitators who wrote these chapters are willing to let go of didactic knowledge transmission, and instead embrace constant feedback from their students and graduates to improve their methodologies. While each contributor has considerable knowledge and experience, they have found that listening and reflecting on their students' needs yields the strongest results. This was particularly salient in Kirby's, Penaluna's (Chapter 15), and São Simão's (Chapter 17) words. Penaluna also points out the value of inviting former graduate successes to return to speak about their 'real-life' experiences to current students, highlighting how their previous course has benefitted them. They can also offer mentoring support to students from a place of familiarity, not fear. As Elbert Hubbard[6] asserted "The greatest mistake you can make in life is to be continually fearing you will make one."

RISK AND FEAR

Penaluna observes entrepreneurship as a complex risk pursuit, where students need to make authentic decisions and deal with consequences and failure. The defeat of student fear, particularly of failure, is one that comes up repeatedly in this section, alongside thoughts on how to inspire resilience and teach intelligent risk-taking. Trust in the educator develops less risk adverseness as the student learns contextually from failure.

Educators themselves often take risks in developing interventions for diverse cohorts of students, for which there is no one size fits all. In looking to develop grit and resilience within his graduates,[7] Maritz (Chapter 14) also observes the importance of a supportive institution, not that pays lip service, but one that is action orientated.

We are working against a backdrop of criticism and challenges for what is observed to be a 'Dark Side of Entrepreneurship Education'[8] with an assertion of dangers and unintended consequences to students and universities. Amongst the risks are students aspiring to start ventures, when they are insufficiently prepared. Thus, the entrepreneurship educator is charged to develop the enterprise competencies, prior and in parallel with the technical process of startup.

Knowledge of the impact of business failure on family and communities, underpin Penaluna's convictions that students have an emotional comprehension and connection with their affordable loss/risk.

TOOLS

Whilst maintaining momentum for the development of enterprising skills and mindset development as discussed in the first two sections, the venture creation process necessitates training into the technical and the science of entrepreneurship. For many programs entitled 'entrepreneurship' this is the initial entry point for a learner interested in pursuing the study, especially if they already have an idea to exploit.

There are tools with robust theories behind them put forward, from Kirby's use of self-managed teams, to Maritz's encouragement to learn from case study 'failures'. They provide practical solutions that would be beneficial to any group wanting to advance the skills needed to become an effective entrepreneur. Both Martitz and Kirby highlight that it is the approach to the use of the tools that is more important that the tools themselves.

One such tool is equipping learners with the skills of developing a business plan and a pitch, as a delivery vehicle for entrepreneurship education, for which Burns[9] observes:

> I wish I had a pound for every excellent business plan produced by an MBA student with absolutely no intention of starting their own business. As I discovered with my business, knowing what to do is far easier than actually doing it.

However, Kirby's chapter provides testimonials from his students as to how his approach to the compilation of a plan, in enhancing understandings of the process, inspired startups from those who had not previously considered it. Where there is consensus amongst all the contributors, is that action-orientated experiential learning is crucial and that reflection is the key to unlocking its full potential. Thus, the long-held assertion of Mezirow,[10] remains true "reflection enables us to correct distortions in our beliefs and errors in problem solving. Critical reflection involves a critique of the presuppositions on which our beliefs have been built".

Whatever practice our educators adopt, the use of 'flipped classrooms', reminds us that many 'new' initiatives have been around long before the terminology was invented. In the same vein Penaluna posits that Lean Startup,[11] effectuation[12] and, more obviously design thinking[13] have their roots in the traditions of design education.

Another interesting theme that places this volume boldly into 2022 is that the results of the facilitator and the students' work aren't necessarily judged by the traditional standards of constant coursework and examination. São Simão points out the importance of understanding how and why your students work in the way they do before evaluating them – while one may excel at essay writing, another may only shine when asking questions of the work. Maritz places importance on student self-reflection, though always makes a wide array of tools and activities available, dependent on the context. Penaluna even mentions laughter as an indicator of classroom success, as relaxed cognition has been known to stimulate creativity.[14] As creativity leads to innovation, São Simão, highlights the importance of learners having an understanding of intellectual property rights in order to protect it.

Each of the contributors to this section bring an abundance and diverse 'real-life' experience to the chapters they have written. Suntola, for example, is a musician, while Maritz is a former executive director in the entertainment industry. What this adds to this collection of essays, and is enforced by the contributors, is the importance of learning by doing. This means different things to different contributors, from pitching in front of a class of supportive peers (as São Simão encourages) or in a simulated online entrepreneurial environment. Each approach offers something to learn – but the shared approach they all agree is that you must do it to benefit from it. What is essential is that the experience is authentic, in that you know who you are as an educator and why you made that choice of practice.

NETWORKS

The eco-system of support, with social capital within the graduate's networks were observed to be essential. This ranged from facilitating multidisciplinary meetings where learners identify co-founders with which to explore a concept, through to accessing finance. It was therefore seen to be incumbent upon facilitators to maintain synergistic relationships within their eco-system. As Csikszentmihalyi[15] observes:

> College teachers are important in two ways. First, they can ignite a person's dormant interest in a subject and provide the right intellectual challenge that leads to a life-long vocation. Second, they often exert themselves in various ways to make sure that the student is noticed by other important members of the field.

CURIOSITY

John Dewey[16] further noted that

> with respect then to curiosity, the teacher has usually more to learn than to teach. Rarely can he aspire to the office of kindling or even increasing it. His task is rather to keep alive the sacred spark of wonder and to fan the flame that already glows. His problem is to protect the spirit of inquiry, to keep it from becoming blasé from overexcitement, wooden from routine, fossilized through dogmatic instruction, or dissipated by random exercise upon trivial things.

Curiosity is another attribute both possessed by the contributors and encouraged by their teaching approaches from their students. Suntola notes that when her learners start asking questions fearlessly is when she is sure they will stride towards success, while Penaluna places much value on her shift in approach towards being a curious facilitator, as opposed to the inflexible, less effective lecturer that she started out as.

LESSONS LEARNED

All the contributors have in some way progressed their way of thinking about entrepreneurship due to interactions with their students, graduates' educator networks and research. It seems one must keep ahead of the curve in order to transmit the passion for entrepreneurship these contributors plainly have in huge amounts, and to teach in the most timely way.

Perhaps the most surprising anecdotes that some of these educators share is that they have experience of past institutions that they have worked in that deny the value of entrepreneurship education, even going so far as to shut down conversations about supporting its development with their own staff (see Penaluna and Kirby's depressing testimonies for proof). In considering the theories and experiences we can only hope those who shunned this demonstrably valuable practice are feeling more than a little embarrassed. All of these attributes overlap in various ways from each contributor's viewpoint, making their diverse experiences a feast of food for thought for those both new to the field, and for existing practitioners.

NOTES

1. QAA (2018).
2. See Bosna et al. (2020).
3. See Nabi et al. (2017).
4. See HESA (2020).
5. See Hamel (2012: 248).
6. See Hubbard (1927: 151).
7. See Maritz (2020a).
8. See Bandera et al. (2020).
9. See Burns (2018: v–vi).
10. See Mezirow (1991: 1).
11. See Ries (2011).
12. See Sarasvathy (2008).
13. See Martin (2009).
14. See Ziv (1976).
15. See Csikszentmihalyi (1996: 185).
16. See Dewey (1910: 34).

14. Guiding your entrepreneurial journey
Alex Maritz

Entrepreneurship is living a few years of your life like most people want, so that you can spend the rest of your life like most people can't.
(Anonymous)

I have a background in technology disruption and commercialisation. I was fortunate to spend a decade or two as an Executive Director as a corporate entrepreneur with Sony Playstation and Ster-Kinekor (country licensee for the likes of Sony Pictures/Columbia Tristar, Disney, Universal Studios, 20th Century Fox and Paramount). I was part of the executive team that disrupted the gaming market and we introduced the DVD format to home entertainment. This eventually revolutionised the home entertainment market, opening new sales channels and ultimately closing huge chains such as Blockbuster Video and Video Ezy. I then entered academia, a result of my passion for life-long education and development of people and markets. My mentorship, question-ing of status-quo, calculated risk-taking knowledge and skills, and mindfulness that start-up failure isn't necessarily a bad thing, most influenced my active engagement and approach to entrepreneurship education and facilitation. My corporate leadership lead to me doing a double bachelors degree in psychology and business management, then an MBA in strategy. I subsequently completed my PhD in entrepreneurship. I have been in my academic role close to 20 years, mostly in a learning and teaching, research and engagement role as a Professor of Entrepreneurship. I have been fortunate to actively collaborate in global entrepreneurship ecosystems, having spent lots of time at start-up facilities across the USA, EU, China, Taiwan, Japan, Russia, Africa, Latin America and even Iceland. This involved my integration as a global Google Start-up facilitator. I believe in a theory-for-practice perspective and that the best way to predict the future is to create it.

MY FACILITATION PHILOSOPHY

I could tell you all about the generic mumbo jumbo, such as experiental learning, activity-based learning, enquiry-based learning, all great concepts, but are these suited to guiding your entrepreneurial learning, surely something more dynamic is required? In fact, does entrepreneurship education actually enhance successful start-ups? Then again, what is a successful start-up? And if you fail in a start-up, is that really a bad thing? What about learning from failure? After all, failing is the first attempt in learning, right? What about risk, can you add value or even disrupt if you are risk averse; maybe calculated risk is the answer? Getting back to failure, what are the root causes of failure, and how do we overcome them? And once students launch their venture or start-up, how do they grow or accelerate it? Do they take on a mentor, if so, what does that mentor do? Who other than the start-up entrepreneur guides the entrepreneurial journey?

So what is my teaching/facilitation philosophy? Well, it evolves and changes, just as the dynamic ecosystem changes.[1] I need to adapt and use the latest tools, even create the latest tools. Currently it's about dynamic facilitation and being a start-up navigator, guiding the entrepreneurial journey. Disruption creates space for entrepreneurs; hence I adopt disruption in my entrepreneurship education and facilitation.

MY CONTEXT

As a Professor of Entrepreneurship, first and foremost, I am responsible to guide our university students along their entrepreneurial journeys, being it delivering on entrepreneurial intentionality or even entrepreneurial self-efficacy. This includes facilitation at Bachelor, Masters and PhD level. I'm also fortunate to be involved with the University Accelerator, an award-winning incubator of ideas and commercialisation. This is a tad different to my entrepreneurship education facilitation and entrepreneurship education program within the university, it's a lot more dynamic. More like Google start-up weekend! Then I also do many workshops to nascent and experienced entrepreneurs, on things such as learning from failure, lean start-up, business model design, design thinking (ok, this is getting a bit long in the tooth now), dynamic risk management, growing ventures, harvesting/exiting ventures and the like. But all in all, it's about navigating start-ups and guiding their entrepreneurial journey. I also specialise in minority entrepreneurship, with special interests in senior entrepreneurship and Indigenous entrepreneurship. Boom or bust may amplify my approach to context within the Australian entrepreneurship ecosystem.[2]

My Ideal Graduate

The entrepreneurship graduate that I am trying to develop is that person who is willing to develop authentic grit, the elusive (but essential) entrepreneurial trait.[3] By this I mean the passion and perseverance associated with the pursuit of challenging goals that awe and inspire nascent and experienced entrepreneurs to succeed emotionally, take positive risks and be true to their cause.

Why this Type of Graduate?

These graduates may not only become entrepreneurs now or in the future, but may become game changers. Their enterprising skills may well facilitate this, becoming what they are truly capable of becoming. This may even include entrepreneurial intentionality and/or entrepreneurial self-efficacy. I believe whether you have ambitions for entrepreneurship or just remaining relevant in the workplace, having or building enterprising skills is seen as an imperative. At their most basic, enterprising skills encompass resourcefulness and initiative. Others include commercial awareness, decision making, innovative thinking, problem solving, strategic thinking, working independently and communication skills. Further, just think how skills such as creativity, digital and financial literacy, presentation skills, building effective relationships, critical thinking and teamwork provide logic of why students would benefit from using these skills.

My Theories of Development

I certainly have a theoretical approach to navigating start-ups. I believe in entrepreneurship education scholarship, based on research. As mentioned, I am a firm believer of a theory-for-practice sake perspective. Just like entrepreneurs, I learn from failure, that way I keep abreast of the latest developments and initiatives in entrepreneurship education and facilitation. I justify my approaches based upon dozens of entrepreneurship education scholarly articles, journals and research that I have developed, written and edited, in addition to participating in dynamic entrepreneurship education workshops with global experts in this domain. In entrepreneurship education, we care and share. I am not a believer in just providing real-life cases in class, but providing a research-led, informative and scholarly robust approach to start-up navigation. Also, I use theoretical concepts on content development; this is particularly the case in the evolving field of senior entrepreneurship. It's interesting that this is the fastest growing sector of entrepreneurship and start-ups. Senior entrepreneurship is often seen as the driver of social innovation.

DEVELOPING ENTREPRENEURIAL VENTURES

My approaches regularly change, as transformation necessitates change and adaptation. Currently, I'm sold on Dietmar Grichnik and the teams approach to start-up navigation.[4] This includes profiling, prototyping, sourcing and scaling in guiding the entrepreneurial journey. I will elaborate on how I implement this from perspectives of learning from failure, risk alternatives, mentorship and overall start-up navigation. I then provide inference on how I apply this using mini-cases within an Australian context. There are, of course, specific pedagogies and methods to enhance entrepreneurial intentionality and/or entrepreneurial self-efficacy, and as importantly, creating value.[5]

The reason I have adopted the Grichnik navigator approach is that it combines content, pedagogy and process in an easy and systematic way. Whilst it's not a paradigm shift, it does combine other approaches of enterprise skills, lean start-up, design thinking and business model generation. It also aligns to my own approaches such as authentic grit, intentionality and self-efficacy. Here's a very brief overview of the navigator approach:

Profiling. Includes the individual entrepreneur, motivation, the customer, problems/pains, jobs customers need to get done and solutions or gains, solving the problem. Aligns very well with my frameworks of opportunity evaluation. Students complete a start-up cockpit.

Prototyping. This includes the product/service offering, value propositions, go to market, the unfair advantage and competition. I integrate lean start-up here, with a few components of business model design. Students identify metrics, KPIs and unit economics.

Sourcing. This is dynamic integration, team roles and competencies, networks and partners, co-creation, call to action, risk compass, value chain requirements, and of course, intellectual property. I align the entrepreneurial ecosystem to this section, plus other components of business model design. I also add learning from failure, mentorship and risk assessment.

Scaling. A vital component many entrepreneurs do not prioritise. This includes investment, how much cash is required before you earn. It's about defining growth strategies and managing the growing business. And ultimately, the main identifier of entrepreneurship as a process, the deal and exit, or harvest, as many of my colleagues refer to it. This may include finding an appropriate investment partner. Okay, so this method has yet to be tested for effectiveness, but it's not a one shop approach. As mentioned, I adopt and adapt the navigator approach, keeping up with the times. It's about replication and extension, learning from failure. Remember, to fail is the first attempt in learning!

Stages of Development

Well, one size doesn't fit all, there are more problems and more answers, which in turn enhance divergent thinking, as promoted by Jones and the

Penalunas,[6] which include nurturing the creative, innovative and entrepreneurial mindset, taking into account educational constraints and challenges (and we certainly have many of these), from pedagogy to andragogy to heutagogy, capacity-building across traditional boundaries, engaging role models, aligning the learning to the task, evaluating unpredictable implementation/s, and finally, understanding how emotion impacts on learning and performance. Components of entrepreneurship education programs have to be constantly updated and validated, from outcomes to pedagogy to participants.[7]

Evaluating Outcomes

This involves a myriad of initiatives and approaches. Learning 'about' entrepreneurship may enhance intentionality, and I use analytical texts and knowledge retention in this regard, for example, a report on an entrepreneur of choice. Learning 'for' entrepreneurship is more about self-efficacy, necessitating students to demonstrate their development, moving onto learning 'through' entrepreneurship, primarily a reflective process, where a student engages in entrepreneurial activities and maps their own learning and supported progression.[8] I use a range of measures and initiatives suited to specific contexts, such as knowledge retention, knowledge harvesting, teamwork, managing unknown outcomes, start-up pitches, business model design, incubation/acceleration measures and input, mentorship and portfolio analyses. Having an appetite for calculated risk and failure provides a conduit for innovation and creativity, which I evaluate throughout the entrepreneurship process.

Areas of Student/Graduate Difficulty

I find students grapple most with uncertainty, failure and a risk appetite. Obviously mediation is required, particularly in risk-averse institutions such as universities. I also find that students' own career goals and aspirations impact how far they wish to progress into the enterpreneurship space or zone. Some even have fear that others will 'steal' their intellectual property, something I alleviate right from the start. Student learning experiences are also diverse, so effective and ongoing support needs to be contextualised in a range of different ways. After all, it's about the entrepreneurial mindset, entrepreneurial effectiveness, entrepreneurial competencies and entrepreneurial awareness. These are dynamic concepts and certainly not linear, therefore my open-minded and iterative approach.

My Challenges

We must remember that entrepreneurship is not for all, hence a broad under-standing that only 1 in 10 people globally participate in start-up activity. But for those that don't, we may enhance entrepreneurial intentionality but embrace enterprising behaviour. For those that dipped their feet in entrepreneurial behaviour, or those that have failed in start-ups, we may enhance entrepreneurial self-efficacy. But it's important to recall that entrepreneurs do not fail, but their start-ups may. This is because most start-ups take place in high-risk scenarios. It's about embracing enterprising skills, and adapting these skills to different and challenging environments. My decision making may not always be supported by critical analysis, synthesis and judgement, but tends to rather be focused on resilience and flexibility when faced with change or uncertainty.

Nature of Confirmation

I get back to authentic grit, that is what I strive for in my facilitation. Just how well students portray this grit provides me with efficacy of my approach/es. How well students identify and respond to stakeholder needs, how well they critically reflect upon solutions, how well they integrate digital and data skills, how well they visualise the future, how well they develop critical reflection, how well they apply resilience and adaptability and how well they manage resources to intuitively make decisions under uncertainty provide me with a wealth of confirmation of my efforts.

SHARED WISDOM

Entrepreneurship has the bonus of being significantly multi-disciplinary, hence the opportunity to add value across varied and wonderful contexts.[9] Furthermore, entrepreneurship may be seen as an enabler to economic activity, specifically during/after challenging times, such as was experienced during the COVID-19 pandemic.[10]

These contexts are fully transferable to corporate scenarios, particularly through leadership and management, action and reflection, communication and strategy, digitalisation and new innovations. My facilitation is not limited to high-growth start-ups, but changes in the entrepreneurial mindset, facilitating different kinds of entrepreneurship, such as youth entrepreneurship, gender entrepreneurship, social enterprise, senior entrepreneurship, Indigenous entrepreneurship and technology entrepreneurship.

My Development

I have learned that a supportive institution has a lot to do with entrepreneurship impact. Entrepreneurship is not about lip service, but rather action orientation. I have worked for an institution that supports entrepreneurship (education) university-wide, and others that merely tick boxes. Many encourage student engagement and entrepreneurial outcomes in the learning process, drive graduate success through entrepreneurship and self-employment, articulate institutional development through the entrepreneurial university and strengthen entrepreneurial ecosystems with businesses and social enterprise, alumni and similar ecosystem participants.[11] These are the type of institutions that you should be associated with!

Lessons Learned

Lessons learned, well, that may be divulging my secrets. I'll get to the point. Mix with successful people and institutions. If an institution is a hand-brake to entrepreneurship initiatives, it's probably best to move on. Associate with disciples of the entrepreneurial university and entrepreneurial ecosystem,[12] those that have entrepreneurship embedded in their strategic intent. If it's difficult to move on, at least have an affiliation to such innovative and progressive institutions, find like-minded entrepreneurship alliances!

NOTES

1. See Belitski and Heron (2017).
2. See Maritz et al. (2019).
3. See Maritz (2020a).
4. See Grichnik et al. (2020).
5. See Jones et al. (2014).
6. See Jones et al. (2014).
7. See Maritz (2017).
8. See QAA (2018).
9. See Maritz (2020a).
10. See Maritz (2020b).
11. See Maritz et al. (2021).
12. See Belitski and Heron (2017).

15. Learning from learners and leading from the back

Kath Penaluna

I came here to learn to draw and paint – not learn business studies.
(Anon, 2nd year, Swansea Institute of Higher Education (SIHE) Fine Art student, 5
October 1997)

Tell them from me – they need to know this stuff.
(Anon (same) SIHE, Fine Art graduate, 6 February 1999)[1]

At the age of 18, having convinced the bank manager interviewing me that my skills could move his branch up the regional football league, I commenced a 20-year career in banking, which culminated in various management positions. It was a time when managers made autonomous context-based decisions to develop their branches. Mine was recognized for high lending levels and corresponding low debts. The promotions, that followed the successes, came with long hours and travel, which were not conducive to bringing up a young family. I took advantage of a redundancy opportunity, with clear plans to return within a few years.

Running concurrently to banking, I ran a design business with my husband, Andy, a design educator who shaped his curriculum to include business acumen. Hence, I often joined his classes to share experiences, and supported those taking forward their own businesses. Hearing that I had left the bank and aware of my positive contributions with Andy's students, I was invited by the Dean of Art and Design to deliver 'Professional Studies,' a core module at level 5 (2nd of three years) across the disciplines in 1997. So, without ever having any aspirations to venture into education, my journey began.

MY FACILITATION PHILOSOPHY

My philosophy is aligned with Whitehead's[2] view that 'Education is the acquisition of the art of the utilisation of knowledge.' You might anticipate that the 18-year-old me was confident in both her football skills and in articulating her prowess. On the contrary. I did not play football and it was shyness, exacerbated by the reverence with which the 'bank manager' was held within her community, that prevented me contradicting her assumptions. Reflecting on the interview with friends, who were eager to know how I got the job above far more academically qualified candidates, afforded me many lessons. The most powerful one was that pushing aside assumptions and wise questioning is essential for meaningful collaboration and empowerment.

Ignoring my own advice, I assumed that all Art and Design students would value business expertise from a bank manager and co-manager of a design studio, so I delivered my tutelage through the traditional transmission of knowledge that I had experienced within my own Business School education. It was a quick lesson into there being no 'one size fits all' approach to entrepreneurship education. The 150 students I was faced with could be placed on a continuum of extremes. Design students tended to observe that they wanted more understandings, while fine artists wanted none of it. The challenges faced, as exemplified by my graduate quotations commencing this chapter, led to my being a curious facilitator. Exploration and co-creation for context-relevant approaches underpin my philosophy. It harks back to that intellectual skill of questioning, which I see in successful educators and entrepreneurs.

MY CONTEXT

I am the Enterprise Manager at the University of Wales Trinity Saint David (UWTSD), which is a merged institution encompassing the aforementioned SIHE. It's a position I have held since 2005, when I transitioned from lecturing in entrepreneurship across the disciplines, to having responsibility for the infrastructure of support for student, graduate, and staff startups. It is a triple helix approach for innovation, with academia, industry and government working collaboratively to foster economic and social development. Since 2019, I have been the Director of the International Institute for Creative Entrepreneurial Development (IICED), which was launched under the Directorship of Professor Andy Penaluna in 2014. Integral to my role is being a Welsh Government (WG) Entrepreneurship Champion. WG provide funding to Further and Higher education institutions in Wales for a single point of contact to develop and report on initiatives and impact. It is an intervention unique to Wales and the associated stakeholder engagement is integral to my provision.

I endeavor to implement structures and cultures across our varying campuses; three in Wales and two in England, that balance stability and flexibility. Graduate ventures are established at the intersection between entrepreneurial thinking and deep discipline expertise.

My Ideal Graduate

Whatever their discipline, my ambition for our graduates is that their experiences, scholarly knowledge and learning lead to being curious, imaginative, connected contributors, who are kind and wise, inspired and inspiring.

Like many post-1992 HE institutions, we celebrate widening participation from within our local communities and seek to actively break down barriers to education. Thus, for many of our learners, connecting them to networks of people to enhance their own social capital, in turn, augments an understanding of their own offering within organic structures and dynamics. As much learning takes place from and with others, this requires social intelligence, not just recollection ability. My ideal student or graduate can think on their feet and use what they have learned thoughtfully.

Why this Type of Graduate?

Learners are motivated and guided by their own values, be they ethical, cultural, or faith-driven principles, and these determine their priorities. Social intelligence, and the art and science of persuasion and influence are emotional competencies for any endeavor,[3] so when they can combine these with their discipline of choice, they are already part way on the ladder to success.

Motive and emotion share the same Latin root 'motere' meaning 'to move,' and it is emotional drivers that will shape their actions as they pursue their goals. This means the kind of sense check that I mentioned earlier. As these graduates make their own life decisions, they need to actively seek out as many opportunities as possible to give them flexibility when things change.

These graduates are rarely stuck in their own discipline, as they can see the value of other studies and consider the thoughts and ideas of other people. When we review our startup numbers and question why we are consistently highly ranked for this in the UK, especially when it comes to survival rates, I always come back to this ability to see connections with other people and other approaches.

My Theories of Development

My approach is constructivist, with our learners constantly adding new knowledge to prior experiences and learning. Within a classroom environment my tools are problem-solving and inquiry-based learning activities, encouraging the forming and testing of ideas. It is experiential, with deep reflection core to the learner's discovery. Heutagogical (self-determined learning) approaches are designed to develop learners' autonomy and capacity to deal with complexity, as they challenge their own assumptions and gain insights into how they learn, in addition to what they are learning.[4] I aspire to deliver information imaginatively, to fuel the curiosity within my learners, as observed by Whitehead,[5] 'Imagination is not to be divorced from the facts: it is a way of illuminating the facts', and 'a fact is no longer a bare fact: it is invested with all its possibilities'.

DEVELOPING ENTREPRENEURIAL VENTURES

Critical informants are my entrepreneurial alumni, a network of some 700 graduates running their own businesses. These alumni are contributors to the student journey. Initially, this is by raising awareness of entrepreneurship as a career choice by contributing to curriculum delivery. Their willingness to engage automatically leads to them being amongst graduates' network of support, especially as ideas for ventures unfold. It is of note that in addition to their own expertise, these alumni make introductions to their own networks as befits the business needs.

My entrepreneurial alumni are my most powerful 'tools'. It is this mutual learning and sharing of context-relevant expertise, with graduates who have started their own ventures, that informs my developments. They fuel my drive for continuous improvement, a journey that they generously travel along with me.

Stages of Development

I now look to develop in all of our learners the competencies aligned to the European 'de-facto' guidance EntreComp,[6] and the pre-requisite 21st-century skills of creativity, team-working, critical thinking, opportunity recognition and problem solving. In turn, the personality traits of being flexible and adaptable, and capable of coping with ambiguity and risk are developed too. The UK's Quality Assurance Agency's guide is my number one 'go to'.[7]

As I support delivery across all disciplines, I understand where development is core in a discipline, and is already so firmly embedded that it is omnipresent. There is no point in trying to teach what their subject is already rather good at: making it relevant becomes the key. By way of example, innovation starts with creativity which is at the very heart of an art school, so you are unlikely to find a module called 'Creativity and Innovation'. Yet they are developing advanced divergent as well as convergent thinking skills that, combined with discipline-specific and multi-disciplinary understandings, leads to innovation.

My learners are regularly joined by role models, who share experience and expertise beyond inspirational anecdotal evidence of their successes, to also expose learners to the practicalities of 'failures' within the process and their emotional impact. As an entrepreneur and bank manager I witnessed first-hand the devastating impact of bankruptcy on founders, their families, and the communities they supported. I believe it unethical to espouse entrepreneurship as an ultimate goal, but an option by design, or necessity, for which learners need an understanding of risk, not in an abstract way, but with a realization of their own affordable loss.

Evaluating Outcomes

Within the curriculum, formative and summative assessment varies across the disciplines, and responds to the needs of its specialist stakeholders. For learners this spans portfolios of work, public presentations, and the production of artifacts, through to examinations prescribed by professional awarding bodies. The aim is for the learner to be provided with authentic assessment practices for which tutor observations and grades are provided in a feed 'forward' as opposed to feed 'back' methodology.

My interventions are designed to respond to Norris Krueger's observations of the centrality of mindset development and the importance of the entrepreneurial ecosystem. Thus, I evaluate engagement and participation in activities, and as laughter demonstrates relaxed cognition, it is encouraged. As learners become more adept, they are able to see more potential solutions to problems and are more capable of redefining the problems avoiding the 'Premature Articulation' of rushing to first thoughts. The entrepreneurial ecosystem, developed over twenty years, facilitates engagement with multiple stakeholders with diverse expertise and resources to support the nascent entrepreneur's journey.

Areas of Student/Graduate Difficulty

When I first became an educator, I provided the answers to the question – or what I perceived to be the question – and therefore gave the 'notionally correct answer'. But as my own understandings developed, I saw the power of questioning as fundamental to student learning. I adopted a technique used by Andy (Penaluna), whereby he would respond to learners' questions with questions to provoke further interest, stimulating and challenging the learner. It took me years of practice to hone that skill, of responding with questions that motivate the learner to discover more, not sate the thirst for knowledge that I was previously quenching in order to fulfill the need to pass examinations where answers are already known. This presents challenges for learners who are not used to such an approach; they can be frustrated at a lack of being given 'the correct answer'.

Using wicked problems to which there is no correct answer helps learners to see beyond this obstacle, especially when they are future-orientated, and no individual can claim absolute certainty. The alumni help with this enormously, as their tasks are believed, and insights valued. Whilst talking of value, asking learners to place a monetary value on work produced for assignments provides a platform for them to get used to costing and estimating as much as possible, based on their own productivity.

My Challenges

The terms enterprise, entrepreneurship, entrepreneurial, and employability were convoluted and used interchangeably until the UK Quality Assurance Agency guidance was published in 2012 and the high level of support became apparent in the review for 2018. The problem was mainly with academics, and less so with entrepreneurs, so there are synergies and distinctions that are helpful to clarify from the outset.

My greatest challenge is the clock, with whom I have regular battles whether in a classroom or authoring strategy documents, grant applications and pre-senting business cases to varying stakeholders for re-framing or re-forming practice. I find it ironic that within education, progression means a reduction of direct teaching hours in favor of administrative undertakings. It's a huge challenge of prioritizing, as opportunities for advancing compete with imple-menting solutions for day-to-day issues. Thus sadly, I sometimes skip on the metacognition, 'thinking about thinking,' that I advocate for my learners.

Nature of Confirmation

UWTSD has been ranked number 1 in Wales and number 2 in the UK for graduate businesses running for three or more years.[8] We are also ranked consistently highly for number of startups. Their success rates tell an engaging story, especially when taking into consideration that we have relatively low student numbers.

This suggests that our approaches work, but it is the interpretation of these metrics that is fundamental. When it comes to causation, I'd highlight that my colleagues and myself are interested in our alumni journeys and welcome staying in touch with them. Arguably therefore, it is the fruitful relationships and the corresponding alumni engagement that is captured and reflected in these statistics. Moreover, it is the alumni observations that we consider to be the best in terms of critiques.

We also have an ever-growing ecosystem of support, growing in terms of the expertise and associated resources. Our enthused expanding network is another indicator of success. Simply put, people in business are seeking us out, and surely that is an indicator in itself?

SHARED WISDOM

Entrepreneurial alumni consistently reaffirm the value of experiential learning and deep reflection. My learners are encouraged to experiment and to reflect upon their actions and the associated outcomes at all stages of their development, but there is a cautionary tale to share. To move the learner beyond what they anticipate the tutor is looking for within a reflective piece, particularly if there are grades attached, takes both practice and mutual trust. I recall a colleague whose grades were influenced by his perception that the reflection piece should clearly relate to the positive impact of their intervention, so other insights were missed.

Entrepreneurial alumni abound, but few universities use this valuable resource. Alumni returning to their programs of study to deliver workshops, have been shown to be far more impactful than introducing a 'heroic' entrepreneur; they can relate their comments to the subject being studied and link their studies effectively to what they have learned beyond graduation. Likewise, their mentorship of those starting ventures commences from common ground, with mutual understandings for meaningful collaboration. My main message is one I was offered early in my teaching career: become a student of your past students.

My Development

Key to my development is the increasing understanding that the Business School has a big part to play, but rarely should it be the leading actor. Almost every discipline has a strength to build upon first. Ventures are driven by imaginative, curious people, with creative, innovative ideas, who have the knowledge, skills, and behaviors to progress. This necessitates multi-disciplinary understandings, which can be encouraged through inter-department and interdisciplinary learning.

The development of business acumen can be introduced once innovative competencies are recognized within disciplinary subject areas. From that sound base, the authoring of a business plan, or the development of an elevator pitch to attract funding, becomes far more relevant and far worthier of a learner's attention.

I started back to front by 'delivering' lectures on things like cash flow and marketing theory, but soon learned the error of my ways. There are many watershed moments, and one springs to mind immediately because I questioned myself before going too far down the wrong track. Why was I teaching pitching and persuasion to performing arts students who were well ahead of me at this, for example? They could act so well and take on so many character roles in such a persuasive way already!

Lessons Learned

I've learned that theories are important tools in our armory, but I don't confine myself to literature anchored in US Business and Management Schools. I've explored cognitive psychology for learning and motivation, sport for good practice in coaching, engineering for insights into product and service development, and computer science for using big data and visualization techniques. Many approaches espoused for startup, such as the iterative user-centered approach of 'Lean,'[9] the resource decision making of 'Effectuation,'[10] 'Value Creation Pedagogy'[11] and more overtly 'Design Thinking'[12] already have roots in design's overarching aim to utilize creativity to solve other people's problems, thus their underpinning literature has helped me to learn in much greater depth.

Whilst theories inform and reinforce my practice, it is the expertise within the ecosystem that guides my thinking, in particular entrepreneurial graduates. They teach me to capture the motivation and drivers for each venture being taken forward as a key component of contextual understandings. It is this network of graduates who regularly remind me of the multi-disciplinary facets of running a business, and that passion is the central tenet for success, however achievements are measured.

Have conversations with colleagues within and beyond your usual domain: those that you find good company and with whom you can share mistakes as well as successes. Your influencers should bring you joy as well as wisdom with a nod to a few of mine; Margherita Bacigalupo, Allan Gibb, Colin Jones, Norris Krueger, Harry Matlay, Elin McCallum, Fiorina Mugione and Andy Penaluna. I have learned over the years that mistakes, whist painful at the time, can be useful anecdotes to support your messaging further down the line. I was particularly aggrieved when in liaising with my Head of the Business School, at that time, I was given short shrift and advised that enterprise education had no place in a business school. It has provided the fodder for many a debate ever since.

NOTES

1. Comments by an alumna, initially whilst a Fine Art student and subsequently as a graduate and professional artist.
2. See Whitehead (1929: 6).
3. See Goleman (1999).
4. See Jones, Penaluna and Penaluna (2019).
5. See Whitehead (1929: 97).

6.   See   EntreComp   https://ec.europa.eu/jrc/en/publication/eur-scientific-and
      -technical-research-reports/entrecomp-entrepreneurship-competence
      -framework.
7.   See QAA (2018).
8.   Higher Education Statistics Agency (2020).
9.   See Ries (2011).
10.   See Sarasvathy (2008).
11.   See Lackéus (2016).
12.   See Martin (2009).

16. Developing the harmonious venture

David Kirby

The many environmental and social problems that now loom large on our horizon
cannot be solved by carrying on with the very approach that has caused them.
(HRM, The Prince of Wales[1])

When I went to university, my intention was to become a teacher – but on
graduation, I obtained a state scholarship to study for a doctorate and entered
the academic profession in a research capacity. I missed teaching, though,
and applied for lectureships in subject areas and locations where I could
specialise in my field of interest: the contribution of indigenous small firms to
regional economic development. My first lectureship was in Wales, and I was
determined to bring to my teaching the most enjoyable part of my education,
my Doctorate. This had been essentially a period of experiential learning.
I began to experiment in the classroom and found that most students enjoyed
and benefitted from it. At the same time my research showed that most small
firms do not grow, so I began to offer training programmes using the same
experiential learning techniques used with my undergraduates. These were
also well received.

MY CONTEXT

My facilitation philosophy is very much based on learning by doing,[2] and
I discovered that this is the way entrepreneurs prefer to learn also. In terms of
Honey and Mumford's[3] four preferred learning styles (i.e., activist, reflector,
theorist, and pragmatist) the entrepreneur has a preference for the activist and
pragmatist while academia traditionally favours the reflector and theorist.
This would suggest that if we are to create graduate entrepreneurs, we need
to encourage our students to adopt a more activist and pragmatist approach.
Also, it goes some way towards explaining why so many entrepreneurs do not
succeed in the education system. However, I found there is another factor to
be considered: brain hemisphere dominance. Research in South Africa[4] has
shown that successful entrepreneurs have a right brain learning preference,
whereas the education system is essentially left brain. Again, this would
help explain why so many entrepreneurs fail educationally, but it would also

suggest that if entrepreneurship education is to help create entrepreneurs, we need to develop the right brain thinking skills of our students by encouraging them to think creatively, intuitively, and emotionally. This is very different from the logical, rational, objective, detached traditional left-brain approach to learning. Thus, my facilitation philosophy, presented in Kirby (2003) and (2007), is experiential learning in which the student is exposed to Activist and Pragmatist learning and encouraged to develop right brain thinking skills.

The harmonious entrepreneurial venture is one that addresses not just the economic challenges facing society (wealth creation and job generation) but the inter-connected environmental, humane, and social problems that constitute the sustainability challenge. In recent years, the traditional economic approach to entrepreneurship has been complemented by ecopreneurship,[5] humane entrepreneurship,[6] and social entrepreneurship.[7] The Harmonious venture, exemplified by Egypt's Sekem Holding,[8] integrates or harmonises all four approaches. In 2003 Sekem received the Right Livelihood Award (the Alternative Nobel Prize) for the way it combined 'profitability and engagement in world markets with a humanistic and spiritual approach to people and respect for the natural environment ... a business model for the 21st century in which commercial success is integrated with and promotes the social and cultural development of society through the "economics of love".

If entrepreneurship is to address the challenge of sustainability, harmonious entrepreneurship is applicable to all economies and societies. During Global Entrepreneurship Week in November 2020, Felicity Healey-Benson and I launched The Harmonious Entrepreneurship Society[9] in order to promote the concept, support entrepreneurship educators, and equip young adults with the knowledge, competences and skills to launch a Harmonious entrepreneurial venture.

My Ideal Graduate

The ideal graduate is someone who can see an opportunity and take responsibility for bringing it to fruition, and in the process bring about change and improvement. They will think and behave like an entrepreneur and will be able to cope with uncertainty and ambiguity, make sense out of chaos, initiate, build, and achieve. While the student will know how to launch a commercially viable new venture, and be able to do so, they will also possess a concern for the environmental and social problems that constitute the sustainability challenge. In addition to the traditional business and personal competences of the entrepreneur, therefore, the ideal graduate will need to have:

• ethical, environmental, and social consciousness.
• a concern for people and the ability to motivate and empower them.

- an understanding of systems thinking.
- the ability to think strategically.
- the ability to be both a visionary and activist.

Several of these competences have been recognised previously by Lans et al.[10] and more recently by Ploum et al.,[11] but in addition, our research[12] identified the importance, also, of spirituality: the holistic belief in the individual's connection to others and to the world as a whole. This is a tenet of Islam, the religion of the founder of Sekem, Professor Ibrahim Abouleish. However, it is also a feature of most of the leading world religions and is fundamental to, for example, the notion of Stewardship in Judaism, while in the Bible[13] we are told 'the Lord took the man and put him in the Garden of Eden to work it and take care of it' (Genesis 2: 15). Hence spirituality and a sense of inter-connectedness with the rest of humanity and nature, may be, therefore, an important added attribute.

Why this Type of Graduate?

Both students and society benefit. Students benefit from acquiring both the knowledge and skills to launch a new harmonious venture, and the skills and competences sought by employers. Society benefits too, as although new forms of entrepreneurship have been developed (such as ecopreneurship, social entrepreneurship and humane entrepreneurship), they do not address the sustainability problem per se, though it has been recognised that entrepreneurship has the potential do so.[14] Indeed, classical economic entrepreneurship can have negative consequences, particularly for the environment and society since the sustainability challenge is multi-faceted, embracing interrelated economic, environmental, and social concerns. This means that efforts to address one facet will have implications for all others. As Popper[15] has observed, 'every solution of a problem raises new unsolved problems'.

In accordance with Ashby's Law of Requisite Variety,[16] therefore, any potential solution needs to be equal to or greater than the number of factors involved. Thus, if entrepreneurship is to help resolve the sustainability problem it has to provide a holistic, integrated solution that does not address just one facet but all four – economic, environmental, humane and social.

My Theories of Development

I believe, strongly, that education has placed far too much emphasis on knowledge acquisition and the passing of assessments. Often such an approach relies heavily on passive learning and rote memorisation. Apart from its academic limitations, in an era of unprecedented uncertainty,[17] society needs 'to release and support the skills of men and women who can envision and push innovations' as Moss Kanter[18] has recognised. This is what I am attempting to do. At the same time, I believe that although citizens in a global economy are inter-dependent, we are required, increasingly, to take ownership of our own destinies, which suggests that individuals, communities, organisations and even societies need to develop a greater sense of enterprise and self-help.

DEVELOPING ENTREPRENEURIAL VENTURES

Stages of Development

My students work in, preferably, multidisciplinary teams. The first stage is to learn about team formation, including selecting a leader and identifying the different team roles each member will play.[19] This stage involves various self-assessment exercises including the Durham University General Enterprising Tendency test.[20] The teams then embark on the second stage which is identifying the new venture – often referred to as ideation, a medical term referring to the forming of mental images. They then start to pass through the first of Tuckman's five phases of team development.[21] By the end of this stage, the teams have usually navigated the Forming and Storming phases and reached the Norming phase. They now embark on the Performing phase which has to do with:

- undertaking the requisite research to construct a rigorous, realistic plan for the venture to determine its feasibility and commercial viability
- identifying the resource needs of the venture including potential sources of funding
- raising finance and launching the venture.

Throughout this stage the teams, which are basically self-managed,[22] are monitored and mentored, required to network, and keep records of their contacts, and encouraged to monitor on a 'feel wheel' the periodic emotions of their members. Once this stage has been reached it is not the intention that the teams will pass into the Adjourning phase of Tuckman's cycle, but many teams do. Whether they break up or continue, the final stage is reflection – what has been learned, what skills have been acquired and what are the members' plans for the future?

The launched ventures are further monitored and supported with the aid of a negotiated agreement or contract that becomes the action or learning plan[23] for the next stage in the venture's development. It outlines what needs to be done or learned, and how and by when it will be done, thereby giving the founder(s) ownership of the learning and ensuring it is relevant and timely.[24]

Evaluating Outcomes

Various evaluations are used, including peer appraisal, presentations to expert panels, and formal assessment of the written components of the programme, particularly the business plan. Throughout, the participants are expected to reflect on what they have learned and the skills they have acquired. The number of ventures created and launched is not used to evaluate, as the aim of the programme is to educate the participants about entrepreneurship and develop in them the attributes of the entrepreneur. Not every participant is suited to self-employment and not every idea that is generated is viable commercially. It is important for students to learn this and make appropriate career choices.

The development of the entrepreneurial mindset is felt to be a more important objective. It will serve the students throughout their lives and could result in the launch of a new harmonious venture at a later, more appropriate, time. As one student put it, 'I need to work first in an organisation that encourages entrepreneurship to get more experience before starting my own business.' However, another student who went on to launch his own venture on graduation and won a USAID entrepreneurship competition claimed that the module not only provided the basis for his new venture but was 'one of the most important modules a student should have studied'.[25] Hence, the major evaluation outcome of the programme is how the students believe they have benefitted from it.

Areas of Student/Graduate Difficulty

The greatest difficulty for students comes, I believe, at the outset of the programme. Rarely have they experienced anything similar in their educational journey. As one student acknowledged, 'I believe the course is really valuable and unique compared to other core courses. What makes it unique is that it aims to focus more on developing the student.' While both the content and the process, particularly the emphasis on the Activist and Pragmatist approaches to learning, comes as a shock to many, most adapt and enjoy the experience, finding it challenging, motivating and beneficial.

One student who did not initially like being required to think in front of the class, apparently told her uncle, a successful entrepreneur, of her worries. His response was, 'all that counts in your life is your ability to present and think under pressure, you will be thankful for such a professor one day'. While this is itself motivating, the educator also needs to be motivated and entrepreneurial. You must 'infect' your students with the entrepreneurial virus through your love of the subject. Inviting young, successful entrepreneurs to address the class helps tremendously with this, particularly if they are recent alumni.

My Challenges

In the early days, there were those who did not believe entrepreneurship could be taught. There were even academics who did not believe it should be taught, especially as part of the curriculum. Universities have changed, but such people do remain. I overcame them by persevering, offering extra-curricular programmes, receiving external funding, and obtaining third-party endorsement.

My more recent challenges deal with the nature of Higher Education, in particular the rigidity of the timetable, traditional design of lecture theatres (even in some of the newer institutions), the teaching of subjects in single discipline silos, and the adherence to traditional methods of assessment. In one institution, I was not allowed to use a learning 'contract' in case the students sued the university, while in one education system I was not permitted to teach outside of my academic discipline or to change the curriculum and improve it. It had been approved and therefore had to be taught. Such bureaucracy and lack of imagination is being eroded, gradually, but it will only disappear if we educators are bold enough to innovate, make mistakes and learn.

Nature of Confirmation

The evidence that the course works comes initially from an early version that received an award for the way it 'developed the personal competence and confidence of its participants and for the way such a high proportion of those participants turned their academic knowledge and skills into successful products and businesses of their own'. On one occasion, I received an endorsement from a colleague in another institution. I took one of his graduates back to the institution from which he had graduated. I wanted him to act as my Graduate Entrepreneur. After his presentation, his tutor congratulated him, and said to me, 'I don't know what you have done, but he is a different person.'

However, perhaps the efficacy of the course is best demonstrated by the students themselves and their feedback. While one student recognised that all universities should allow students to start ventures on campus, another pointed to the way the course had, 'opened my eyes to a different aspect of life. It helped me to explore my own capabilities in terms of thinking in an entrepreneurial way.' While two others acknowledged the practical benefits:

> The course was very beneficial and gave us a boost of motivation to look more into being our own people.
> The reason [we] are writing this together is that we both decided to actually start planning a project together after graduation.

Perhaps the most poignant endorsement, though, came from a Computer Science student who claimed the course:

> Practically spoke to me. I'm at heart an entrepreneur. It gave strength to those who know they're not reckless and irresponsible just because they want to follow their dreams.

SHARED WISDOM

I have taught entrepreneurship and new venture creation successfully in the UK, Asia, Europe, MENA, Scandinavia, South Africa, and South America, and have trained educators both in the UK and internationally. I was also a founder of the EU-funded European Doctoral Programme in Entrepreneurship,[26] a consortium project led by the Autonomous University of Barcelona intended to train future academics how to teach and undertake research in the field. Many of the participants are now successful university entrepreneurship educators.

My Development

The most important thing to learn is that you are not the source of all knowledge, but part of the learning community – you learn with your students and need to be open to new ideas. You should encourage them to find out for themselves and help break the dependency culture by not allowing them to become dependent on you. You are a facilitator of their learning.

Lessons Learned

In the modern knowledge economy, universities are the catalyst for economic and social development. Access to knowledge is as important in the 21st century as access to raw materials was in the 19th century. Accordingly, universities have acquired a third mission involving the transfer and commercialisation of the intellectual property derived from the research of their academic staff and students. While many institutions have adopted this third mission and become more entrepreneurial, there remains opposition to its development.[27] If you are faced with this in your institution, do not be deterred. Become more determined. Look for ways to overcome the opposition – seek allies, funding, sponsors, and third-party endorsements of your efforts and remember, you are part of a global movement, so join such recognised networks as ICSB, ISBE, and EEUK.[28] But your greatest allies are your students – they will support and promote you.

Don't despair. Seize the day!

NOTES

1. See HRH The Prince of Wales, Juniper and Skelly (2012).
2. See Kirby (2003).
3. See Honey and Mumford (1986).
4. See Nieuwenhuizen and Groenwald (2004).
5. See Kainrath (2011).
6. See Kim et al. (2018).
7. See Borzaga and Defourny (2001).
8. See Abouleish and Kirchgessner (2005).
9. See https://harmonious-entrepreneurship.org/.
10. See Lans et al. (2014).
11. See Ploum et al. (2018).
12. See Kirby and El-Kaffass (2021).
13. See Genesis (2: 15).
14. See Villar and Miralles (2019).
15. See Popper (1963: 44).
16. See Ashby (1968).
17. See Peters (1987).
18. See Moss Kanter (1984: 354).
19. See Belbin (1981).
20. See Caird (2006).
21. See Tuckman (1965).
22. See Kirkman and Rosen (1999).
23. See Stephenson and Laycock (1993).
24. See Kirby (2007).
25. See Kirby and Humayun (2013).
26. See Urbano et al. (2008).
27. See Kirby (2020).
28. Specifically, the International Council for Small Business (icsb.org), The Institute for Small Business and Entrepreneurship (isbe.org.uk), and Enterprise Educators UK (enterprise.ac.uk).

17. Defending open culture in facilitation, research and entrepreneurship

Fátima São Simão

I have been working with ventures in the creative and cultural sector for almost twenty years now. I engaged in many artistic and cultural activities in college. One of my most defining experiences was the period I became president of the University of Porto's theatre group, TUP. Not only was it a fundamental experience in terms of testing and applying the tools and theories I was studying at the Faculty of Economics, but it was also the starting point of my professional pathway. Being engaged in the arts from an early age helped me understand some of the main challenges and problems artists and cultural workers face, but it also gave me a broad range of unexpectedly useful tools to work with students, young professionals and entrepreneurs. As a business developer at UPTEC Science and Technology Park of the University of Porto, I also soon found out that such tools were not only useful within cultural and creative sector projects: they were powerful in virtually every venture.

MY FACILITATION PHILOSOPHY

My philosophy is sharing knowledge. I try to promote an open culture as much as possible. This is nothing new or unique. And, as I discovered recently during my PhD research, it is even a trend. As Manuel Castells[1] puts it, power is no longer in information collection but in information flows. Or, as some cultural economists keep reminding us, in the digital era, content is no longer king – distribution is.[2]

Such an open attitude towards sharing or 'distributing' knowledge also comes from an urgency to change our current economic paradigm, motivated by the growing general sense of social, cultural and environmental responsibility. Working with students, young professionals and entrepreneurs in such demanding times makes one constantly recalibrate values, needs, goals. The global COVID-19 pandemic reminded us we live in a common and limited ecosystem, where everything can have an unpredictable impact. Now more than ever, the challenges ahead are unimaginable. It is in our hands, as facilitators, individuals, and societies, to try to ask the right questions and share them with our students, so we can search for answers together.

MY CONTEXT

For the past twelve years, I have been working at UPTEC Science and Technology Park of the University of Porto. Created in 2007, UPTEC fosters the development of business projects in the sciences, arts, and technologies, by sharing knowledge between the university and external stakeholders. We do this through supporting knowledge-based startups to grow within an ecosystem of innovation centres (from SMEs to major multinational development teams) and an intensive programme of activities developed with business experts, students, and researchers. Initially, startups go through a pre-incubation programme where they confront and develop their ideas in constant discussion with their cohort peers. Guidance and support is also available from UPTEC's team of business developers and from a vast network of resident entrepreneurs and external partners. After this six-month period, the startups begin their incubation programme, with access to internal activities and benefits that support their growth, always in articulation with the university and its stakeholders. I also teach Media Economics at the University of Porto to undergraduates and Masters students.

My Ideal Graduate

Every graduate is ideal in their own specificities and skills. And, ideally, what I wish is to be capable of enhancing those virtues and helping them overcome or assume their difficulties. Every student and entrepreneur is very different from another. And the most extraordinary things happen when you actually contribute to their recognition of their own capacities and interests. This is often visible when they work in teams and realise that what they think they cannot achieve is completed perfectly working with one another. As facilitator, you are not there to mould anyone but to facilitate their discovery of themselves and the world around them. Another exciting moment is when you realise they are losing that initial shyness and start asking questions – especially so-called 'ridiculous' questions. They no more expect to be guided, they actually take the lead of the conversation and guide you – the facilitator – through what they wish to learn and understand.

Why this Type of Graduate?

Students are professionals in progress. But they are also citizens in progress. More than making sure that they are able to use all tools and know all theories, it is important that they know where to search for them and, again, that they don't fear asking questions. Critical thinking comes from existing knowledge but also from discussion and sharing of ideas. Understanding that there are many different perspectives of the same idea, in the same way there are many possible pathways to their professional careers and many different business models, is fundamental. It is crucial that they (and we) understand that decisions have consequences, and they might not even be possible to guess. Stimulating their curiosity and their sense of responsibility towards their own context and the world in general is always important. Regardless of if they become more or less active citizens, it is important they know their decisions have an impact in the world.

My Theories of Development

The theoretical basis of my approach is in academic research methodologies that provide tools to observe, experiment and question the world around us. Authors such as Hannah Arendt,[3] Pierre Bourdieu[4] or Howard Becker[5] influence my work as researcher, facilitator and business developer. Also, artists, from Joseph Beuys[6] to Samuel Beckett, to Marina Abramovich have always been inspiring and defining to my approach. But maybe even more than well-known giants, many close professors, students, entrepreneurs, and friends continue to inspire me. It is important to know the history of things, and to understand that you are not inventing anything – someone, somewhere probably already thought or even wrote about what you are only now discovering.

DEVELOPING ENTREPRENEURIAL VENTURES

Whatever kind of session I am dealing with – be it a graduate level lecture or a workshop for entrepreneurs – I always try to understand who my audience is: where they are from, why they come to this class, and what their interests are. This helps me choose my materials. I like to mix different instruments. There is always a strong theoretical basis. Such theory is related to tools, films, videos, gifs, or memes (openly licensed) and case studies. Often, such case studies come in the form of a testimony, given by experienced professionals that I invite to come and share their thoughts and practice. Continuous dialectic between theory, practice and media helps reinforce understanding of the main ideas, as students get the chance to explore and question things by themselves.

Another important instrument is group work: by working in teams and having to defend their own position towards a collective goal, students rapidly understand the power of good argument and the importance of negotiation. They also have fun. If the learning (and teaching) process becomes fun, it becomes way more effective too.

Close communication is also desirable. This means you are available to share materials and opportunities you find, not only during class time. And, in times of crisis, it means you can show your solidarity and vulnerability towards a situation that is hard on everyone, and to which you don't have all the answers.

Stages of Development

Resistance: Often students start by resisting this kind of methodology. At first, some might even think you are only trying play the 'cool' facilitator or you really don't know what you are talking about.

Relation: As you start introducing more theoretical references and inviting practitioners to present their own perspectives, they start to relate the materials with their own experiences and knowledge and usually become more interested and inquisitive. Depending on the size and diversity of students and respective interests, the main challenge is to find a correspondent diversity of examples and materials that they can relate to.

Appropriation: As you put them to work in groups and circulate around each team to answer their questions and help them resolve their conflicts, the ownership process begins, and you can observe how much they have appropriated the tools you have been discussing. It is usually easy to understand their commitment by observing the work they do outside the classroom.

Integration: At the moment of presenting the results of their work, be it through more practical demonstrations (doing a pitch) or through more theoretical arguments (in a written or oral exam), you finally see them integrating the concepts and instruments they have learned. Absolute integration is recognisable among students who get back to you after the end of the course or workshop asking for recommendations about how to continue their work or giving suggestions to improve the programme.

Evaluating Outcomes

All students have different personalities, so I try to adapt my evaluation methods as a continuous reflexive evaluation process. It is very important to understand who your audience is before you implement any evaluation method. Some students will respond very well to debates. Some others are better at writing an essay. Others only show their learnings outside the classroom (through comments and questions they send by email, for example). Observation is essential to evaluate any kind of knowledge sharing. It not only reveals the situation of the students, but it is also a very effective mechanism of self-assessment. It allows you to understand if your performance corresponds to the demands of the group. I introduce exercises that allow the student to test their learnings, as I monitor my teaching.

Group work is usually assessed at a pitch session, where each team presents their project using the instruments and techniques they have learned and tested in class. This is an open session, anticipated by commented rehearsals. When it is possible, I invite one or two experienced professionals to participate as a jury. Their comments can also be considered in the final evaluation.

Areas of Student/Graduate Difficulty

As in everything anyone does professionally, knowing who you are doing it for is fundamental. Knowing your students, asking them where they come from and what are their interests helps to minimise eventual difficulties. If you understand who they are, individually and as a group, you can adapt your programme. Of course, there will always be students who will not cope. But this is often due to personal reasons, which is why it is so important to get to know them. Some students are far from home, some live with their families, some come from privileged backgrounds, others make a lot of effort even to attend the classes, for example, because they have a job or children to take care of. All of this interferes in their learning process, making it more or less difficult. If you remain available to consult throughout their learning process, it is much likely that you can overcome difficulties together – both theirs and yours.

My Challenges

Again, I'd say the biggest challenge is to understand the group I have in front of me and, with time, to learn them. This requires effort and focus, not only in trying to understand who is who, but also in trying to adapt your programme to their needs. Each group means you need to select different materials, different guest speakers, different projects, different juries, and mentors. And this is also why it is so important to have a strong theoretical basis: if everything goes wrong you have enough knowledge to replace instruments and materials. My background in theatre and my close work to artists and creative entrepreneurs also helps, as I have learned to improvise and be creative. To teach is to share knowledge but it is also to perform. A lot of knowledge without performing skills may become dull, and an excellent performance without solid knowledge may become ridiculous. None of this works without structure. A good balance between these three axes – knowledge, performance, and structure – is key.

Nature of Confirmation

From the growth of creative startups, to the successful implementation of cultural projects, or the rapid professional development of graduates, there are many examples I could number as successful results of my work. However, such results are not mine. I only contribute to them. I am very aware that I typically work with young adults that have already paved a way to get where they are when I meet them. I am very keen on making that evident to them. I am a facilitator and the only serious indicator I consider as a proof of efficacy of my approaches is when a new group of students in your optional course comes into the classroom or when the new young entrepreneurs bring in a new project or when that email from an old graduate falls in your mailbox saying "we made it!" or "we failed it". It is when people you have shared your knowledge with share it back that you realise your approach works. And this is why it is so important to remain available beyond the classroom or mentoring session and promote an open culture of continuous knowledge sharing – not just knowledge transfer.

SHARED WISDOM

The approaches I have followed and tested have proven to be effective in many different contexts. The essential methodology is the same but, as explained before, the model is adapted to each different group. Depending on their interests and motivations, the structure of the programme will include more or less technical or theoretical content and the performance will vary between mentoring and lecturing. In any context, the structure is never too rigid.

In short, the basic structure works as a script, which can be longer or shorter, more theoretical, or technical, depending on the audience. And, although the essential knowledge areas covered are pretty much the same, the examples, tools and case studies chosen to illustrate and transfer them will vary.

My Development

One of the most important things I have learned (and continue to learn) is that there are always many different ways to look at something. I come from an economics background, always in strong relation to the arts. For a long time, I did not understand how they could be combined. When I found out that they could, it was a eureka moment. I had felt prejudice from many economists I knew about my artistic universe, and later also felt the same kind of judgement by many artists about the fact I was an economist. That told me a lot about closed silos and how important it is to let yourself be inspired by people who think differently from you. Working in a science and technology park with the mission of developing cultural and creative business and projects within technology and science startups has only contributed more to this belief. I have observed many different mindsets and ways of reasoning and seen the amazing things they do when put together, as long as they are valued and respected.

Lessons Learned

From my experience, the best ally to any kind of facilitation (and practice) is knowledge. I am a strong advocate for education and culture. In this respect, universities are an institution in which independency needs to be defended and celebrated. Experience is also fundamental, of course. Theory will probably not be enough if you don't experiment, in practice, what it means and how it applies. This continuous dialectic between theory and practice is fundamental.

On the other hand, looking for alternative and even contradictory perspectives is also important. Working around the concept of business models, intellectual property and strategy in the cultural and creative industries, in my case, meant I had to go through PhD research to understand the structures and dynamics of the sector and how copyright was influencing them. This led me, for example, to find the amazing alternatives that open licensing can offer to entrepreneurs when designing their business models and freelance strategies. On the other hand, it helped me have a much clearer view of the relationship between economics and the arts. This knowledge, combined with my professional practice, contributed to the development of specific tools (such as the Creative Commons Toolkit for Business (2019) or the Concentric Circles Model of Cultural Work) that I now use as facilitator. Studying and researching to improve one's own knowledge and being open to share, discuss, and question it is not only personally gratifying but is also strategic and effective, not just to facilitators but also to students, entrepreneurs and any other professional in search of answers yet to be questioned.

NOTES

1.   See Castells (2005).
2.   See Towse and Handke (2013).
3.   See Arendt (1958).
4.   See Bourdieu (1982).
5.   See Becker (1998).
6.   See Beuys and Bodenmann-Ritter (2007 [1972].

18. What can we learn from the arts for creative entrepreneurship?

Silja Suntola

Traditionally, entrepreneurial training has focused on developing enterprises, not entrepreneurs as human actors.[1]
(Hägg, 2011)

My background is in music (MMus/Arts Management, BM/Music Production/ Engineering). I worked in the music business as producer, engineer, musician, teacher, and entrepreneur for over ten years with numerous talented and successful artists. It certainly had its moments. Long and hectic working hours, multiple sources of income and a level of uncertainty was stressful to balance by the time family life came into the picture.

When family took precedence, I took up a position in education development at a music university, shifting my focus to national and international development projects. I continued to the art university, starting to address students from all art sectors. Next, I moved onto Aalto University Small Business Center and South-Eastern University of Applied Sciences to further creative industries and entrepreneurship in any sector, though still mainly through research and development projects.

Artists and creative people set trends rather than follow them. They question presumptions, often coming up with something we hadn't even considered. If science and technology answer the question 'how?', art and artists deal with the question 'why?'. If science can be calculated through numbers and formulas, art is sensed, felt, and heard within our body, mind and soul. This is something that rings true for creative entrepreneurship too.

MY FACILITATION PHILOSOPHY

Much of my philosophy stems from the variety of roles and positions I've held in my working life. On one hand I've been an entrepreneur and freelancer, on the other an educator and developer within arts, business, and multi-disciplinary contexts, and including interacting with policy makers. Experiencing different positions and sides of the industry has given me perspective, something I value and try to pass on. Just like a painter steps back from a painting before working on the details, taking space to reflect is a core skill in entrepreneurship.

Human-centric thinking and doing is another central skill. In training I invest time to think and discuss issues like identity, values, and sense of meaning in their relation to entrepreneurship. We figure out what one wants to do and achieve in life, what things are more important than others, and why. It is about both personal and professional development: we humans come in one package.

A side of creativity that is often forgotten is letting go. In order to build something new, you often have to get rid of something old. That might be beliefs, ideas or thinking habits, or a creation that has come to be dear and seemingly indispensable. Letting go and just starting from scratch can be tough, but often essential for something new to be born.

MY CONTEXT

My work is mainly within research and development, which means most activities are part of continuing education, lifelong learning and piloting new curricula and programs. Courses might range anywhere from three to thirty or more days. One example might be a special course for groups of people that have been made redundant, or one for adult learners that have just started nurturing the idea of becoming an entrepreneur.

Research and development projects frequently allow piloting new approaches to learning. They can include skills in facilitating multi-disciplinary groups and networks, project-based work in 'living lab' type of environments or testing hybrid models of online and offline activities.

Currently the COVID-19 crisis has provided an overwhelming need for online learning. This shift in people's mindset towards working online opens numerous opportunities for new learning, teaching, and facilitating approaches, globally.

My Ideal Graduate

Courses realised within different research and development projects are much about piloting and testing, so participant groups often differ by background. Technical criteria or requirements (prior studies demanded etc.) are often given, so such criteria refer more to qualitative aspects, and I value:

- Motivation for professional and personal development. Openness and curiosity. Readiness to try new approaches and peer-to-peer learning.
- Self-awareness and ability to reflect to develop personally and professionally. Being able to identify and improve on areas that need development.

How to develop entrepreneurial graduates, ideas and ventures

- Positive and constructive attitude. Constructive criticism is valuable, and change doesn't happen without it, but it must be followed by the will to find solutions. Negative attitudes affect the atmosphere in the whole group, which is especially damaging when discussing people's dreams, hopes and fears on their learning path.
- People skills. Peer-to-peer learning and group work is a central element of the training. Being shy or introverted by nature is certainly not a problem (besides, I've seen a number of students transform from silent wallflowers to the most charming presenters or pitchers). Being ready to go beyond one's comfort zone if and when it is needed.
- Passion to change the world for the better – perhaps it's naive, but I get excited when I see people who have a strong inner calling to use their talents to not only fulfil their personal dreams, but to provide real value to society.

Why this Type of Graduate?

Creativity and entrepreneurship are similar in many ways: they're about visioning and creating something that hasn't existed before. Creative and entrepreneurial individuals or groups are willing to go out of their way to take risks and try out things no one has tried out before to come up with solutions. Practise, repeat and try once again, and not always out of pure enjoyment (especially after the sixtieth try...), but out of determination to get there.

Even though some entrepreneurs may state making money is the main purpose of their enterprise, this is often not the case with arts entrepreneurs. For them, entrepreneurship is more of a necessity, a concrete tool for managing finances when traditional jobs in their field of interest don't always exist. And for many entrepreneurs, they invent most of all for the joy of doing something meaningful and to excel and share the excitement of doing it with others, all while making a living. Of course, one can end up very financially successful too.

I enjoy my work most when I see a person or group grow as people as well as professionals. I love to see them find and unfold their potential while discovering who they really are and can do. That's why I try to assess the ones that are there not merely for the credits or even knowledge but find ones with the deeper will to learn and evolve as human beings.

My Theories of Development

My academic background is based mainly in my studies in Arts Management, as well as some studies on organisational management and leadership at the university.

1. Arts Management provided the basic understanding of creative industries and entrepreneurship within the arts.
2. Studying creative leadership gave me an understanding of organisational management and leadership theories, which I mainly studied with the question 'what can we learn from the arts for management and leadership in any organisation?' in mind.
3. My passion is to further multi-disciplinary thinking and co-creation between arts and business, asking the question 'what can we learn from creative industries for entrepreneurship in any field?'

The human-centric approach is well condensed in this quote from my colleague's dissertation: "Traditionally entrepreneurial training has focused on developing enterprises, not entrepreneurs as human actors."

DEVELOPING ENTREPRENEURIAL VENTURES

Having developed training in very different settings and for different participant groups, three core methodological elements seem to remain constant. Beginning or initiation phase:

*   Introduction and getting to know oneself and others. Knowing oneself is the basis of finding one's entrepreneurial identity. In the process of becoming more aware of one's own identity, values and what one finds meaningful, the easier it is to develop needed skills and knowledge, as well as work with others.
*   Team-building requires time for building trust through getting to know each other. The team also functions as an important quick feedback channel to test and co-create ideas and concepts.

Learning-by-doing phase:

*   Doing simple exercises that allow testing initial ideas quickly, and then iterating them. This can mean creating short pitches about your business idea, playing out scenes from customer service experiences, or visualising the outputs of your product of service. Budgets, processes, or equipment needs can be sketched out.

- Case studies by entrepreneurs can be introduced to spur and support the process. Students can be encouraged to find similar cases themselves by Googling or talking to people in the business.

Testing or feedback phase:

- Shifting gears from practising to testing in real life with potential customers.
- Understanding how different target groups experience the service or product. Studying if and how it helps to solve their problem or create the result they might be looking for. Remembering that customers might not always know exactly what they are looking for or they might not have identified how a service or product might be useful to them.
- Using feedback to improve the service or product.

Stages of Development

The initiation stage is really about building trust within oneself and in others. It is important to enforce basic rules regarding showing respect, giving room for different ways of thinking, and confidentiality.

Many learners also seem to deal with issues relating to sharing their ideas with others. As working in teams is a core element of the programs, trust within the group is crucial. If they aren't prepared to share their ideas, there is little anyone can do to help them improve.

Trust is also a key element in the learning-by-doing phase. Trying out ideas that might be perceived as silly or stupid can be terrifying for many. Learning to give and take feedback constructively as well as being ready let go of some ideas are important skills of entrepreneurship. Providing check-ins, inspirational keynotes and informal discussions can boost the process and help lower the stress threshold of trying things out.

The testing phase means taking the service or prototype out of the laboratories to test with 'real audiences' and potential target groups. Even though many creators and innovators seem to have a tendency towards wanting to develop or rehearse 'just a tad more', prolonging the development phase is not a good idea. You start to lose sight of the forest for the trees and start putting your energy into details instead of what matters most.

Evaluating Outcomes

First of all, evaluation should under no circumstances affect how a person sees themselves as a learner negatively. Tests, essays, or other more traditional forms of evaluation certainly have their place in checking where one is knowing the basics, but personal skills, special talents or other creative soft skills are better depicted through different kinds of references, like portfolio-type presentations and demonstrations.

Self-evaluation and reflection are valuable skills that I try to include in the training throughout. These skills are not just for class, but for life. I often have students keep a learning journal during training programs. Also, art itself offers multiple opportunities for reflection (not to mention expression), whether it's through drawing, making music, videos, or films, or just simply taking time to enjoy art at a gallery or museum and contemplate.

I do see a need for HEIs to develop or implement more tools for identifying and validating creative soft skills, as well as skills acquired in non-formal settings. Creative and entrepreneurial skills develop through practice, repetition and learning-by-doing. Theoretical knowledge and frameworks are important elements that support this learning and enable one to see how the different bits and pieces can fit into the bigger picture. They can help to analyse, research, and evaluate different options and learn from the past. They facilitate a balance between reflection and action or learning and doing.

Areas of Student/Graduate Difficulty

When I was working at the Business School, the economists and business professors were often eager to offer their business plan and financial management classes to our artists. We tried this several times. Time and time again, the feedback was crushing. The students would be angry, complaining how they didn't want someone to explain how to work an Excel spreadsheet or produce a picture-perfect business plan.

They wanted to learn how to build a budget in practice, looking at the whole dilemma they were facing in realising their idea. Their budget might include income from several sources like public grants, expected ticket incomes, projects, sponsors and more. Realising this brought up a number of questions related to taxation, regulations and rules in different contexts. They were often hoping for ideas on where to raise the rest of the money from and hopefully secure some salary for themselves in the meantime.

We concluded this had to be tackled from the inside out, embracing the core idea and understand its value and meaning, and then think of how to fund, manage, and market it.

In sum: do not talk about the money first. Money is the means, not the goal. Artists are passionate about their calling, to the point of being prepared to go out of their way to ensure their integrity. First things first.

My Challenges

There is still a strong preconception about artists being really bad in business. Even though this is true to some degree, it is only half the story. Creatives can be extremely imaginative in coming up with ways to realise their artistic projects by mixing different sources of funding, getting enthusiastic volunteers and sponsors aboard for their cause and managing, somehow.

On the other hand, businesspeople are not always enthusiastic about approaching the complex operating environments that most creatives deal with. It's a skill of its own to be able to navigate between the public, private and third sector domains, or to build and lead cross-sectoral networks that share common interests with cultural and social value.

Furthering creativity and entrepreneurship are high on most regional, national, and international agendas. So is cross-fertilisation between arts and business. We need to find a common language and to have some sense of the social and cultural realms of the other. Multi-disciplinarity in general often stumbles on basic and everyday challenges that relate to communication and understanding.

Nature of Confirmation

It is almost impossible to prove direct causal relations between one approach or training and quantity or quality of the resultant entrepreneurial action. I have had the chance to review extensive feedback in numerous training initiatives while being Project Director for Creative Industries Finland, a national coordinator for the ESF Development Programme between 2007 and 2014. CIF's role was to steer, support, mentor and assess the over forty national projects that were financed through the program. Projects were mainly training for creative entrepreneurship, management, production, and internationalisation in the sector.

Even if the projects differed in length, form or context, most positive feedback related to holistic and human-centric approaches. Many involved felt someone took them seriously for the first time as a person, listened to their everyday concerns about making a living as well as understood their passion. Networks and peer support were certainly another element that was highly appreciated.

Certainly, the best feedback has been from individuals who have come back years later to speak about some of the revelations they gained about what they want to do with their lives, and then go on to inspire people around them at the same time.

SHARED WISDOM

A key element of creative entrepreneurship is a human-centric approach, along with understanding and skills based on creative methods, processes, and people. These can be divided into:

- Creative technical skills. This refers to methods like visualisation; using images, artefacts, or symbols to convey messages; prototyping or building-to-think; presenting and performing; or using skills in storytelling, drama or cultural history and philosophy. Technology offers a variety of possibilities to anyone, requiring little or no skill in the drawing, photography, animation, or video.
- People skills. Increasingly crucial in our multi-disciplinary and networked operating environments. This encompasses bodily communications, cultural understanding, and sensitivity, as well as tools for improving skills for self-awareness, dialogue and communications. Skills in facilitation, coaching and leading creative people and processes in formal or informal settings.
- Learning to learn. The creative process is iterative, developing layer by layer through practice, repetition, and rehearsal. It works as a good model for creative entrepreneurship training. Traditional linear planning tools can be contradictory to the nature of creative processes. Learning-by-doing, project-based learning, and real-life cases are core elements.

My Development

There were times I felt like the wrong person to teach creative entrepreneurship, even though I had my own experience and enough academic studies to lean on. I just didn't feel like I was enough of an expert in the business field.

Even though I had been teaching and training in music production and business, teaching creative entrepreneurship seemed a big leap. But the more I observed different entrepreneurship courses, the more I started identifying themes that seemed to reoccur and related directly to my own experiences in the business. This inspired me to expand my understanding of 'creativity' in entrepreneurship for different contexts.

My role wasn't meant to be a super knowledgeable business wizard, or to have all the tax or copyright laws memorised. It was to identify the core elements, skills, and resources, as well as the attitude that what one doesn't know, one can find out. Thinking for oneself, being realistic without losing passion and fire, or losing it for a while but just figuring out how to find it again are all important. You must do this over and over again, as the learning never stops within our own lives, or that of others and the world around.

Lessons Learned

Being a good facilitator is a skill just like being a good artist or entrepreneur. It takes an entrepreneurial mindset, curiosity, and enthusiasm to keep oneself, and hence others, excited about what one does. Some tips I take to the classroom every now and then:

- Be curious about what is happening around you and the world. Follow the news, read, Google areas of interest and dive into new conversations with others. Have students bring news clips, videos, vlogs… and discuss why and how they are interesting.
- Practise observing and listening every day. Even if we know better, we tend to oversee what might be right in front of us. Turn observing into understanding and hearing to listening. Constantly widen your perspective in order to understand the world.
- On days you can't get your energy up, don't try to hide it too much. People can sense it anyway. Discuss with others how to work through different energy levels. Come up with exercises to brush off the horror of a blank page. Just do it.

Learning is a journey. We don't just learn about things; we transform as people as we become more aware. In the end it's about the little, daily things we do in order to clarify our focus and flame, and to find the facts that help us go where we really want to in life.

NOTE

1.   The citation I chose is from my colleague at Aalto University, Small Business Center, where Outi worked as manager for the university's creative business incubator while finishing her doctoral thesis. Her thoughts really sum up the core element of human-centric development in creative entrepreneurship pedagogy.

References

Abouleish, I. and Kirchgessner, M. (2005), *Sekem: A Sustainable Community in the Egyptian Desert*. Edinburgh: Floris Books.

Aldrich, H. and Kenworthy, A. (1999), 'The accidental entrepreneur: Campbellian antinomies and organizational foundings', in C. Baum and B. McKelvey (eds.), *Variations in Organization Science: In Honor of Donald Campbell*. Newbury Park: Sage.

Allan, D. and Kingdon, M. (2002), *Sticky Wisdom: How to Start a Creative Revolution in Work*. Chichester, UK: Capstone Publishing.

Amabile, T. A. (1998), 'How to kill creativity', *Harvard Business Review*, 76 (5), 77–86.

Ardito, M. (1982), 'Creativity: It's the thought that counts', *Bell Telephone Magazine*, 61 (1).

Arendt, H. (1958), *The Human Condition*. Chicago: The University of Chicago Press.

Ashby, W. (1968), 'Variety, constraint and the law of requisite variety', in W. Buckley (ed.), *Modern Systems Research for the Behavioural Scientist*. Chicago: Aldine Publishing Co.

Bacigalupo, M., Kampylis, P., Punie, Y. and Van den Brande, G. (2016), *EntreComp: The Entrepreneurship Competence Framework*. Luxembourg: Publication Office of the European Union.

Bandera, C., Santos, S.C. and Liguori, E.W. (2020), 'The dark side of entrepreneurship education: A delphi study on dangers and unintended consequences', *Entrepreneurship Education and Pedagogy*, 4 (4), 609–636.

Baron, R. (2006), 'Opportunity recognition as pattern recognition: How entrepreneurs "connect the dots" to identify new business opportunities', *Academy of Management Perspectives*, 20 (1), 104–119.

Barton Rabe, C. (2006), *The Innovation Killer: How What We Know Limits What We Can Imagine – and What Smart Companies Are Doing About It*. New York: McGraw-Hill Education.

Bates, B. (2019), *Learning Theories Simplified* (2nd Edition). London: Sage.

Baxter Magolda, M.B. (1992), *Knowing and Reasoning in College: Gender-Related Patterns in Students' Intellectual Development*. San Francisco: Jossey-Bass.

Becker, H. (1998), *Tricks of the Trade – How to Think About Your Research While You Are Doing It*. Chicago: The Chicago University Press.

Belbin, M., (1981), *Management Teams: Why They Succeed or Fail*. Oxford: Butterworth-Heinemann.

Belitski, M. and Heron, K. (2017), 'Expanding entrepreneurship education eosystems', *Journal of Management Development*, 36 (2), 163–177.

Belsky, S. (2010), *Making Ideas Happen*. New York: Portfolio.

Beuys, J. and Bodenmann-Ritter, C. (2007 [1972]), 'Every man an artist: Talks at Documenta 5', in C. Mesch and V. Michely (eds.), *Joseph Beuys: the Reader*. Cambridge, MA: Bloomsbury, https://s3.amazonaws.com/arenaattachments/74912/Every_Man_An_Artist_-_Beuys.pdf, accessed on 28 November 2021.

Borzaga, C. and Defourny, J. (2001), *The Emergence of Social Enterprise*. Abingdon: Routledge.

Bosna, N., Hill, S., Ionescu-Somers, A., Kelley, D., Levie, J. and Tarnawa, A. (2020), *Global Entrepreneurship Monitor 2019–2020 Report*. London: London Business School, https://www.gemconsortium.org/report/gem-2019-2020-global-report, accessed on 1 November 2021.

Bourdieu, P. (1982), *Leçon sur la Leçon*. Paris: Les Éditions de Minuit.

Bradley, M.J., Seidman, R.H. and Painchaud, S.R. (2012), *Saving Higher Education: The Integrated, Competency-Based Three Year Bachelors Degree Program*. San Francisco, CA: Jossey-Bass.

Bramante, F. and Colby, R. (2012), *Off the Clock: Moving Education from Time to Competency*. Thousand Oaks, CA: Corwin Press.

Brew, J.M. (1946), *Informal Education*. London: Faber and Faber.

Bronfenbrenner, U. (1979), *The Ecology of Human Development: Experiments by Nature and Design*. Harvard: Harvard University Press.

Brown, J.S., Collins, A. and Duguid, P. (1989), 'Situated cognition and the culture of learning', *Educational Researcher*, **18** (1), 32–42.

Bryant, P. (2009), 'Self-regulation and moral awareness among entrepreneurs', *Journal of Business Venturing*, **24** (5), 505–518.

Burns, P. (2018), 'Foreword', in D. Hyams-Ssekasi and E. Caldwell (eds.), *Experiential Learning for Entrepreneurship, Theoretical and Practical Perspectives on Enterprise Education*. New York: Palgrave Macmillan.

Caird, S. (2006), 'Appendix: GET Test 2', in T. Mazzarol (ed.), *Entrepreneurship and Innovation: A Manager's Perspective. Entrepreneurship and Innovation*. Australia: Tilde University Press.

Carey, C. and Matlay, H. (2010), 'Creative disciplines education: A model for assessing ideas in entrepreneurship education?', *Education + Training*, **52** (8/9), 694–709.

Carey, C. and Matlay, H. (2011), 'Emergent issues in enterprise education: The educator's perspective', *Industry and Higher Education*, **25** (6), 441–450.

Carey, C. and Naudin, A. (2006), 'Enterprise curriculum for creative industries students: An exploration of current attitudes and issues', *Education + Training*, **48** (7), 518–531.

Carey, C., Romano, S. and Penaluna, A. (2017), *Insights from the inside; researching creative industries entrepreneurship?*, the 40th Institute for Small Business and Entrepreneurship (ISBE) Annual Conference, Belfast, UK.

Castells, M. (2005), 'The network society – from knowledge to policy', in M. Castells and G. Cardoso (eds.), *The Network Society – From Knowledge to Policy*. Cambridge, MA: Center for Transatlantic Relations.

Christie, M., Carey, M., Robertson, A. and Grainger, P. (2015), 'Putting transformative learning theory into practice', *Australian Journal of Adult Learning*, **55** (1), 9–30.

Creative Commons (2019), *Creative Commons Toolkit for Business*, https://business-toolkit.creativecommons.org, accessed on 1 December 2021.

Creative Industries Council (2020), Facts and Figures/Infographics, http://www.thecreativeindustriescouncil.co.uk/facts-figures/resources-infographics, accessed on 10 March 2022.

Csikszentmihalyi, M. (1996), *Creativity: Flow and the Psychology of Discovery and Invention*. New York: HarperCollins.

Design Council (2007), *Eleven Lessons: Managing Design in Eleven Global Companies, Desk Research Report*, http://www.designcouncil.org.uk/sites/default/

files/asset/document/ElevenLessons_DeskResearchReport_0.pdf, accessed on 1 December 2021.

Dewey, J. (1891), 'Moral theory and practice', *The International Journal of Ethics*. doi .org/10.1086/intejethi.1.2.2375407

Dewey, J. (1910), *How We Think*. Lexington, MA: Heath and Company.

Dewey, J. (1946), *Experience and Education*. New York: The Macmillan Company.

Dewey, J. and Dewey, E. (1915), *Schools of Tomorrow*. New York: E.P. Dutton & Company.

Doris, J. (2015), *Talking to Ourselves: Reflection, Ignorance, and Agency*. London: Oxford University Press.

Dorst, K. (2003), *Understanding Design: 150 Reflections on Being a Designer*. California: BIS Publishers.

Dorst, K. (2011), 'The core for design thinking and its application', *Design Studies*, **32**, 521–532.

Duval-Couetil, N. (2013), 'Assessing the impact of entrepreneurship education programs: Challenges and approaches', *Journal of Small Business Management*, **51** (3), 394–409.

Engeström, Y. (2015), *Learning by Expanding*. Cambridge: Cambridge University Press.

European Commission (2009), *The Impact of Culture on Creativity*. A study prepared for the European Commission, https://keanet.eu/publications/impact-of-culture-on -creativity/, accessed on 30 November 2021.

Fayolle, A., Kariv, D. and Matlay, H. (2019), *The Role and Impact of Entrepreneurship Education*. Cheltenham, UK and Northampton, MA, USA: Edward Elgar Publishing.

Fayolle, A., Verzat, C. and Wapshott, R. (2016), 'In quest of legitimacy: The theoretical and methodological foundations of entrepreneurship education research', *International Small Business Journal*, **34** (7), 895–904.

Foster, J. (2007), *How to Get Ideas*. San Francisco: Berrett-Koehler.

Gibb, A. (2007), 'Entrepreneurship: Unique solutions for unique environments. Is it possible to achieve this with the existing paradigm?', *International Journal of Entrepreneurship Education*, **5**, 93–142.

Goleman, D. (1999), *Working with Emotional Intelligence*. London: Bloomsbury.

Grichnik, D., Hess, M., Probst, D., Antretter, T. and Pukall, B. (2020), *Startup Navigator: Guiding Your Entrepreneurial Journey*. London: Macmillan.

Hägg, G. (2017), *Experiential Entrepreneurship Education: Reflective Thinking as a Counterbalance to Action for Developing Entrepreneurial Knowledge*, MediaTryck. Lund: Lund University.

Hägg, G. and Kurczewska, A. (2019), 'Who is the student entrepreneur? Understanding the emergent adult through the pedagogy and andragogy interplay', *Journal of Small Business Management*, **57** (S1), 130–147.

Hägg, G. and Kurczewska, A. (2020), 'Guiding the student entrepreneur: Considering the emergent adult within the pedagogy–andragogy continuum in entrepreneurship education', *Education + Training*, **62** (7/8), 759–777.

Hägg, G. (2021), 'The entrepreneurial diary – a reflective learning activity to enhance the judgmental abilities of student entrepreneurs', *International Journal of Entrepreneurial Behaviour & Research*, **27** (5), 1142–1165.

Hägg, O. (2011), *Yrittäjyysvalmennus ja yrittäjäidentiteetti*. Doctoral Dissertation. University of Tampere, Tampere, https://trepo.tuni.fi/bitstream/handle/10024/ 66758/978-951-44-8462-9.pdf, accessed on 14 December 2021.

Hamel, G. (2012), *What Matters Now: How to Win in a World of Relentless Change, Ferocious Competition, and Unstoppable Innovation*. San Francisco: Jossey-Bass.

Hansen, D., Lumpkin, G. and Hills, G. (2011), 'A multidimensional examination of a creativity-based opportunity recognition model', *International Journal of Entrepreneurial Behaviour and Research*, **17** (5), 515–533.

Harford, T. (2016), *Messy: The Power of Disorder to Transform Our Lives*. New York: Riverhead Books.

Harford, T. (2017), *Fifty Things That Made the Modern Economy*. London: Abacus.

Heath, R. (1964), *The Reasonable Adventurer*. Pittsburgh: University of Pittsburgh Press.

Hegarty, J. (2014), *Hegarty on Creativity: There are No Rules*. London: Thames and Hudson.

Higher Education Statistics Agency (HESA) (2020), *Higher Education Provider Data: Business and Community Interaction*, https://www.hesa.ac.uk/data-and-analysis/business-community, accessed on 20 November 2021.

Honey, P. and Mumford, A. (1986), *Using Our Learning Styles*. Berkshire: Peter Honey.

HRH The Prince of Wales, Juniper, T. and Skelly, I. (2012), *Harmony: A New Way of Looking at Our World*. London: HarperCollins.

Hubbard, E. (1927), *The Note Book of Elbert Hubbard*. New York: Wise & Co.

Hussain, S. and Carey, C. (2019), 'Lived experiences of female social-housing residents: Stories examining entrepreneurship support needs', *Proceedings of the 42nd Institute for Small Business and Entrepreneurship Conference*, Newcastle, UK, 18–19 November 2019.

Johnson, S. (2010), *Where Good Ideas Come From: A Natural History of Innovation*. London and New York: Penguin.

Jones, C. (2009), 'Enterprise education: Learning through personal experience', *Industry & Higher Education*, **23** (3), 175–182.

Jones, C. (2011), *Teaching Entrepreneurship Undergraduates*. Cheltenham, UK and Northampton, MA, USA: Edward Elgar Publishing.

Jones, C. (2019), *How to Teach Entrepreneurship*. Cheltenham, UK and Northampton, MA, USA: Edward Elgar Publishing.

Jones, C., Penaluna, K. and Penaluna, A. (2019), 'The promise of andragogy, heutagogy and academagogy to enterprise and entrepreneurship education pedagogy', *Education + Training*, **61** (9), 1170–1186.

Jones, C., Matlay, H., Penaluna, K. and Penaluna, A. (2014), 'Claiming the future of enterprise education', *Education + Training*, **56** (8/9), 764–775.

Kainrath, D. (2011), *Ecopreneurship in Theory and Practice: A Proposed Emerging Framework for Ecopreneurship*. Sunnyvale, CA: Lambert Academic Publishing.

Kim, K., El Tarabishy, A. and Bae, Z. (2018), 'Humane entrepreneurship: How focusing on people can drive a new era of wealth and quality job creation in a sustainable world', *Journal of Small Business Management*, **56** (sup.1), 10–29.

Kirby, D.A. (2003), *Entrepreneurship*. Maidenhead: McGraw-Hill.

Kirby, D.A. (2007), 'Changing the entrepreneurial education paradigm', in A. Fayolle (ed.), *Handbook of Research in Entrepreneurship Education*, Volume 1. Cheltenham, UK and Northampton, MA, USA: Edward Elgar Publishing.

Kirby, D.A. (2020), *Entrepreneurial University and Covid-19: Opportunities for Entrepreneurial Transformation? Accreditation Council of Entrepreneurial and Engaged Universities*, https://www.aceeu.org/news/spotlightarticle/id/7, accessed on 1 December 2021.

Kirby, D.A. and El-Kaffass, I. (2021), 'Harmonious entrepreneurship – a new approach to the challenge of global sustainability', *World Journal of Entrepreneurship, Management and Sustainable Development*, **17** (4), 846–855.

Kirby, D.A. and Humayun, H. (2013), 'Outcomes of an entrepreneurship education programme in Egypt: An empirical study of students in Egypt', *International Journal of Management*, **30** (3), 23–35.

Kirkman, B.L. and Rosen, B. (1999), 'Beyond self-management. Antecedents and consequences of team empowerment', *Academy of Management Journal*, **42** (1), 58–74.

Klein, G. (2017), *Seeing What Others Don't*. London: John Murray Press.

Kolb, D.A. (1983), *Experiential Learning: Experience as the Source of Learning and Development*. Hoboken, NJ: Prentice Hall.

Kolvenbach, P.H. (2000), Faith, justice, and American higher education, https://kolvenbach.jesuitgeneral.org/en/archive?view=archivo&id=12, accessed on 1 December 2021.

Komarkova, I., Conrads, J. and Collado, A. (2015), *Entrepreneurship Competence: An Overview of Existing Concepts, Policies, and Initiatives – In-depth case studies report*. Seville: EU Joint Research Centre.

Lackéus, M. (2016), *Value Creation as Educational Practice – Towards a New Educational Philosophy Grounded in Entrepreneurship?* Doctoral Thesis, Chalmers University of Technology, Gothenburg.

Lans, T., Blok, V. and Wesselink, R. (2014), 'Learning apart together: Towards an integrated framework for sustainable entrepreneurship competence in higher education', *Journal of Cleaner Production*, **62**, 34–47.

Last, J. (2017), 'A crisis in the creative arts in the UK?', *Higher Education Policy Institute*, HEPI Policy note 2.

Lehrer, J. (2012), *Imagine: How Creativity Works*. Boston: Houghton Mifflin.

Lewin, K. (1935), *A Dynamic Theory of Personality*. New York: McGraw-Hill.

Maritz, A. (2017), 'Illuminating the black box of entrepreneurship education programmes: Part 2', *Education + Training*, **59** (5), 471–482.

Maritz, A. (2020a), 'Authentic grit: The elusive (but essential) entrepreneurial trait', in C. Jones (ed.), *How to Become an Entrepreneurship Educator*. Cheltenham, UK and Northampton, MA, USA: Edward Elgar Publishing.

Maritz, A. (2020b), 'A multi-disciplinary approach to COVID-19: La Trobe Business School perspectives', *International Journal of Organizational Innovation*, **13** (1), 1–14.

Maritz, A., Nguyen, Q. and Bliemel, M. (2019), 'Boom or bust? Embedding entrepreneurship in education in Australia', *Education + Training*, **61** (6), 737–755.

Maritz, A., Jones, C., Foley, D., De Klerk, S., Eager, B. and Nguyen, Q. (2021), 'Entrepreneurship education in Australia', in C. Matthews (ed.), *Annals of Entrepreneurship Education and Pedagogy – 2021*. Cheltenham, UK and Northampton, MA, USA: Edward Elgar Publishing.

Martin, R. (2009), *Design of Business: Why Design Thinking is the Next Competitive Advantage*. Boston, MA: Harvard Business Publishing.

May, R. (1975), *The Courage to Create*. New York: Norton & Company.

McCallum, E., Weicht, R., McMullan, L. and Price, A. (2018), *EntreComp into Action – Get Inspired, Make it Happen: A User Guide to the European Entrepreneurship Competence Framework*. Luxembourg: European Union.

McLellan, J. and Dewey, J. (1889), *Applied Psychology. An Introduction to the Principles and Practice of Education (1854–1952)*. New York: Educational Publishing Company.

McLeod, F. and Thomson, R. (2001), *Non-Stop Creativity and Innovation*. London: McGraw-Hill.

Mezirow, J. (1991), *Transformative Dimensions of Adult Learning*. San Francisco: Jossey-Bass.

Mezirow, J. (2009), 'Transformative learning theory', in J. Mezirow and E. Taylor (eds.), *Transformative Learning in Practice: Insights from Community*. San Francisco: Jossey-Bass.

Morselli, D. (2019), *The Change Laboratory for Teacher Training in Entrepreneurship Education. A New Skills Agenda for Europe*. Cham: Springer.

Moss Kanter, R. (1984), *The Change Masters: Corporate Entrepreneurs at Work*. London: Unwin.

Mugione, F. and Penaluna, A. (2018), 'Developing and evaluating enhanced innovative thinking skills in learners', in J. James, J. Preece and R. Valdés-Cotera (eds.), *Entrepreneurial Learning City Regions*. Cham: Springer.

Munroe, R. (2015), *What If? Serious Scientific Answers to Absurd Hypothetical Questions*. London: John Murray Press.

Murray, H.A. (1938), *Explorations in Personality*. Oxford: Oxford University Press.

Nabi, G., Liñán, F., Fayolle, A., Krueger, N. and Walmsley, A. (2017), 'The impact of entrepreneurship education in higher education: A systematic review and research agenda', *Academy of Management Learning & Education*, **16** (2), 277–299.

Newton, D. (2012), 'Moods, emotions and creative thinking: A framework for teaching', *Thinking Skills and Creativity*, **8**, 34–44.

Newton, R. (1977), *Reflections on the Educational Principles of the Spiritual Exercises*, https://www.seattleu.edu/media/university-core/files/Exercises.pdf, accessed on 1 December 2021.

Nieuwenhuizen, C. and Groenwald, D. (2004), *Entrepreneurship training and education needs as determined by the brain preference profiles of successful, established entrepreneurs*. Paper presented at the Internationalising Entrepreneurship Education and Training Conference (IntEnt 2004). Naples, 5–7 July.

Palmer, P. (1998), *The Courage to Teach: Exploring the Inner Landscape of a Teacher's Life*. San Francisco: Jossey-Bass.

Penaluna, A. and Penaluna, K. (2008), 'Business paradigms in einstellung: Harnessing creative mindsets for entrepreneurship education', *Journal of Small Business and Entrepreneurship*, **21** (2), 231–250.

Penaluna, A. and Penaluna, K. (2009), 'Assessing creativity: Drawing from the experience of the UK's creative design educators', *Education + Training*, **51** (8/9), 718–732.

Penaluna, A. and Penaluna, K. (2015), *Entrepreneurial Education in Practice – Part 2 – Building Motivations and Competencies*. Paris: OECD.

Penaluna, A. and Penaluna, K. (2020), 'In search of entrepreneurial competencies: Peripheral vision and multidisciplinary inspiration', *Industry and Higher Education*, **35** (4), 471–484.

Penaluna, A., Penaluna, K. and Diego, I. (2014), 'The role of creativity in entrepreneurship education', in Rolf Sternberg and Gerhard Krauss (eds.), *Handbook of Research on Entrepreneurship and Creativity*. Cheltenham, UK and Northampton, MA, USA: Edward Elgar Publishing.

Penaluna, K., Penaluna, A., Matlay, H. and Jones, C. (2013), *When did you last predict a good idea? The case of assessing creativity explored*, Proceedings of the International Small Business and Entrepreneurship Conference, 13 November, Cardiff, Wales.

Peters, T. (1987), *Thriving on Chaos: Handbook for a Management Revolution*. London: Pan Books.

Pittaway, C. and Edwards, C. (2012), 'Assessment: Examining practice in entrepreneurship education', *Education + Training*, **54** (8/9), 778–800.

Ploum, L., Blok, V., Lans, T. and Omta, O. (2018), 'Towards a validated competence framework for sustainable entrepreneurship', *Organization & Environment*, **31** (2), 113–132.

Popper, K. (1963), *Conjectures and Refutations: The Growth of Scientific Knowledge*. New York: Basic Books.

Poynton, R. (2013), *Do Improvise: Less Push. More Pause. Better Results. A New Approach to Work (and Life)*. London: Do Books.

QAA (2012), *Enterprise and Entrepreneurship Education: Guidance for UK Higher Education Providers*. Gloucester: Quality Assurance Agency for Higher Education.

QAA (2018), *Enterprise and Entrepreneurship Education: Guidance for UK Higher Education Providers*. Gloucester: Quality Assurance Agency for Higher Education.

Ries, E. (2011), *The Lean Startup: How Today's Entrepreneurs Use Continuous Innovation to Create Radically Successful Businesses*. New York: Crown.

Roberts, J.W. (2012), *Beyond Learning by Doing: Theoretical Currents in Experiential Education*. New York: Routledge.

Robinson, D. (1990), 'Wisdom through the ages', in R. Sternberg (ed.), *Wisdom: Its Nature, Origins, and Development*. New York: Cambridge University Press.

Roethke, T. and Kizer, C. (2013), *On Poetry and Craft: Selected Prose*. Port Townsend, WA: Copper Canyon Press.

Rogers, C. (1993), *Freedom to Learn for the 80's*. London: Charles Merrill.

Rogers, C. (2002), *On Becoming a Person*. London: Constable.

Romano, S. and Carey, C. (2018), *Collaborative conversation in researching creative industries entrepreneurship; how they contribute to impact and publication*, the 41st Institute for Small Business and Entrepreneurship (ISBE) Annual Conference, Birmingham UK.

Sarasvathy, S.D. (2008), *Effectuation: Elements of Entrepreneurial Expertise*. Cheltenham, UK and Northampton, MA, USA: Edward Elgar Publishing.

Seelig, T. (2012), *Ingenius: A Crash Course on Creativity*. San Francisco: HarperCollins.

Shane, S. and Venkataraman, S. (2000), 'The promise of entrepreneurship as a field of research', *Academy of Management Review*, **25** (1), 217–226.

Smith, M., Moffat, S. and Haynes, T. (2010), 'A Christmas Carol', *Dr Who*, 25 December 2010, at 6 mins and 40 seconds.

Staley, D. (2019), *Alternative Universities: Speculation, Design for Innovation in Higher Education*. Baltimore, MD: Johns Hopkins University Press.

Stephenson, J. and Laycock, M. (1993), *Using Learning Contracts in Higher Education*. London: Kogan Page.

Stewart, S. (2011), 'Editorial: Interpreting design thinking', *Design Studies*, **32**, 515–520.

Sweller, J. (1988), 'Cognitive load during problem solving: Effects on learning', *Cognitive Science*, **12**, 257–285.

Sweller, J. (2015), 'In academe, what is learned, and how is it learned?', *Current Directions in Psychological Science*, **24** (3), 190–194.

Sweller, J. (2016), 'Working memory, long-term memory, and instructional design', *Journal of Applied Research in Memory and Cognition*, **5** (4), 360–367.

Sweller, J., Ayres, P. and Kalyuga, S. (2011), *Cognitive Load Theory*. New York: Springer.

Syed, M. (2019), *Rebel Ideas: The Power of Diverse Thinking*. London: John Murray.

Towse, R. and Handke, C. (eds.) (2013), *Handbook on the Digital Creative Economy*. Cheltenham, UK and Northampton, MA, USA: Edward Elgar Publishing.

Tredennick, H. and Barnes, J. (2004), *The Nicomachean Ethics*. London: Penguin Classics.

Tuckman, B.W. (1965), 'Development sequence in small groups', *Psychological Bulletin*, **63**, 384–399.

Tynan, M. (2017), *An exploration of the suitability of design education approaches in enabling enterprise and entrepreneurship educators to enhance undergraduate students' opportunity recognition attributes, behaviours and skills in Higher Education in Ireland*. UWTSD: Unpublished PhD Thesis.

Urbano, D., Aponte, M. and Toledano, N. (2008), 'Doctoral education in entrepreneurship: A European case study', *Journal of Small Business and Enterprise Development*, **15** (2), 336–347.

Villar, E.B. and Miralles, F. (2019), 'Sustainable entrepreneurship in response to grand challenges: What do we know and how do we move forward?', *DLSU Business and Economics Review*, **28** (3), 102–111.

Virkkunen, J. and Newnham, D.S. (2013), *The Change Laboratory. A Tool for Collaborative Development of Work and Education*. Rotterdam: Sense.

von Hippel, E., Thomke, S. and Sonnack, M. (1999), *Creating Breakthroughs at 3M*. Boston: Harvard Business School Press.

Welter, F., Baker, T. and Wirsching, K. (2019), 'Three waves and counting: The rising tide of contextualization in entrepreneurship research', *Small Business Economics*, **52** (2), 319–330.

White, R.J., Hertz, G.T. and D'Souza, R.D. (2011), 'Teaching a craft – enhancing entrepreneurship education', *Small Business Institute Journal*, 7 (2), 1–14.

White, R., Hertz, G. and Koutroumanis, D.A. (2012), 'Entrepreneurship literacy: The language of the new venture', *Journal of Applied Business and Economics*, **13** (5), 35–45.

White, R.J., Hertz, G. and Moore, K. (2016), 'Competency based education in entrepreneurship: A call to action for the discipline', in C. Matthews (ed.), *Annals of Entrepreneurship Education and Pedagogy*. Cheltenham, UK and Northampton, MA, USA: Edward Elgar Publishing.

Whitehead, A. (1929), *The Aims of Education and Other Essays*. New York: Macmillan.

Zimmerman, B.J. (1990), 'Self-regulated learning and academic achievement: An overview', *Educational Psychologist*, **25** (1), 3–17.

Ziv, A. (1976), 'Facilitating effects of humor on creativity', *Journal of Educational Psychology*, **68** (3), 318–322.

Index

Printed and bound by CPI Group (UK) Ltd, Croydon, CR0 4YY

16/04/2025

14658432-0005